JOURNEY TO
THE COPPER AGE

JOURNEY TO THE COPPER AGE

ARCHAEOLOGY IN THE HOLY LAND

Thomas E. Levy

with photographs by
Kenneth L. Garrett

San Diego Museum of Man
SAN DIEGO

Funding for this publication was provided by

PATRONS OF THE PRADO

Journey to the Copper Age: Archaeology in the Holy Land
was developed by the San Diego Museum of Man and the Israel
Museum, Jerusalem, in partnership with the Israel Antiquities
Authority; National Geographic Museum; and the University
of California, San Diego.

San Diego Museum of Man
1350 El Prado, Balboa Park, San Diego, California 92101

Requests for permission to reproduce material from this volume
should be sent to the San Diego Museum of Man Publications
Department at the above address.

Michelle Ghaffari, *Editor*
Danny Brauer, *Designer and Production Manager*

Printed and bound in Hong Kong
by South Sea International Press, Ltd.

Library of Congress Cataloging-in-Publication Data

Levy, Thomas E.
    Journey to the copper age : archaeology in the Holy Land /
Thomas E. Levy ; with photographs by Kenneth L. Garrett.
        p. cm.
    Exhibition catalog.
    Summary: "Presents early evidence of metal production from
Israel and Jordan, using ethnoarchaeology to document the
discovery and adoption of metallurgy in the Holy Land. This
important development in human history enabled the production
of prestige objects and tools used to build social hierarchies and
facilitate trade"—Provided by publisher.
    Includes bibliographical references and index.
    ISBN-13: 978-0-937808-83-2 (pbk. : alk. paper)
    ISBN-10: 0-937808-83-0 (pbk. : alk. paper)
1. Copper age—Palestine—Exhibitions. 2. Copper age—
Jordan—Exhibitions. 3. Metal-work, Prehistoric—Palestine—
Exhibitions. 4. Metal-work, Prehistoric—Jordan—Exhibitions.
5. Ethnoarchaeology—Palestine—Exhibitions. 6. Ethnoarchaeology—Jordan—Exhibitions. 7. Excavations (Archaeology)—
Palestine—Exhibitions. 8. Excavations (Archaeology)—
Jordan—Exhibitions. 9. Palestine—Antiquities—Exhibitions.
10. Jordan—Antiquities—Exhibitions. I. Garrett, Kenneth L.
II. San Diego Museum of Man. III. Title.

GN778.32.P19L48 2007
933—dc22

                                    2007018221

FRONT COVER: See fig. 3.10, p. 33. BACK COVER: See p. 107.
P. 1: See fig. 5.1, p. 56. PP. 2–3: See fig. 4.7, p. 50.
PP. 4–5: Photograph by Kenneth Garrett, National Geographic,
see fig. 3.23, p. 44. P. 112: See fig. 5.19, p. 66.

CONTENTS

FOREWORD

Journey to the Copper Age: Archaeology in the Holy Land—the book and the exhibition it accompanies—began as a fleeting recommendation by Dr. Michael Hager, chief executive officer of the San Diego Natural History Museum. When Mick introduced me to Dr. Thomas Levy, professor of Anthropological Archaeology at the University of California, San Diego (UCSD), we agreed to discuss the possibility of an exhibition. Little did I know that we were about to embark on a short but intense journey that would lead to a remarkable project.

Three stories intertwine to tell the history of *Journey to the Copper Age*. The first takes place in 1960, when a team of archaeologists from Israel discovered the Cave of the Treasure in the Judean desert. The cave received its name from the incredible contents it held—more than four hundred spectacular prestige objects cast in copper, including crowns and scepters, made over six thousand years ago. The second story is that of a people. The objects in the Cave of the Treasure were created during the Chalcolithic period, or Copper Age (4500–3600 BCE—a time in human development coinciding with the region's first population explosion, the earliest temples, new methods of agriculture, and a progression from making simple implements of wood and bone to controlling fire to transform ore into metals. The third story tells about the art and science of archaeology: the results of research and findings by Levy and an international group of scientists he led on the Ancient Copper Trail expedition of 1997.

One of the great joys of being an anthropologist and museum director is collaborating with scholars to create exhibitions and educational programs based on their research. Like everyone involved in this project, I am grateful to Thomas Levy for all of his efforts and his willingness to jump into a process that attempts to reflect years of his research in clusters of objects, graphics, photographs, and interpretive labels limited to a few hundred words. Adolfo Muniz, graduate student in the department of Anthropology, served as the associate curator and was an indispensable, outstanding member of our team.

Through the generosity of the Israel Museum and the Israel Antiquity Authority, *Journey to the Copper Age: Archaeology in the Holy Land* includes numerous artifacts from the Chalcolithic period, which are being seen outside of Israel for the first time. On behalf of the Board of Trustees of the San Diego Museum of Man, I would like to express our deep appreciation to Dr. Hava Katz, chief curator of National Treasures, Israel Antiquities Authority, for making it possible. It was a privilege to work with the staff of the Israel Museum and we are truly indebted to them for their support. I wish to thank to Dr. James S. Snyder, Anne and Jerome Fisher Director of the Israel Museum, Carmela Teichman, coordinator of curatorial services and traveling exhibitions office; and Michael Dayagi-Mendels, chief curator of archaeology, for their support of this project. Osnat Misch-Brandl, curator of Chalcolithic and Canaanite Periods, served as visiting curator and our liaison for the project in Israel; she was an integral, deeply appreciated member of our team.

The National Geographic Museum made it possible for us to include stunning photographs by Kenneth Garrett; in addition, the museum took responsibility for printing the photographs. Special thanks to Kenneth Garrett for creating these wonderful images. I am grateful to Director Susan Norton, for embracing our vision to create an exhibition that would serve as a public presentation of Levy's scholarly research and for her warm support throughout the process. Thanks also to Cathy Tyson, Billie Leff, John Francis, Wendy Glassmire, and Chris Klein.

We are deeply grateful to the individuals and foundations that have made *Journey to the Copper Age* possible; in particular, Dr. and Mrs. Andrew Viterbi and the Viterbi Family Fund for their expression of confidence early in the project and for providing a matching grant that started the funding. I extend heartfelt thanks to Charmaine and Maurice Kaplan; Dr. Uri Hersher, Skirball Foundation; Earl Feldman Trustee, Novak Charitable Trust; Waitt Institute for Discovery; DLA Piper; Northern Trust; and Patrons of the Prado, Balboa Park; for their generous support. The Jewish Community Foundation was instrumental in our success and we will always appreciate the efforts of Charlene Seidle and Marjorie Kaplan.

It is indeed a pleasure to join Tom in expressing our appreciation to UCSD Chancellor Mary Anne Fox, and Chancellor and Social Science Dean Paul Drake, for embarking with us on this journey to explore the possibilities of presenting to the public the results of scholarly research in a way that makes complex ideas accessible to broad audiences and expands the reach of the work done by ucsd faculty. I also thank Professor Ramesh Rao and the staff of Calit2 for their collaboration. Many thanks to Phil Hoog, who served as exhibition curator, and Kathleen Hamilton, who, with Phil, wrote labels based on Tom's book and insured that the exhibition would be accessible to general audiences. Special thanks to Angela Coleman for creating lovely graphics for the exhibitions, Elle Vitt for managing the final phase of the project, and Sharon Smith and Paul Cleary for raising the funds to make this exhibition possible.

I join Tom in thanking David Mayo, director of exhibitions at the Fowler Museum at UCLA for his wonderful exhibition design. Thank you to Danny Brauer, director of publications at the Fowler, for designing a beautiful book in record time. Danny brought out the best in all of us with his clarity, vision, and good humor. Last but not least, thank you to Michelle Ghaffari for editing the book

Mari Lyn Salvador
SAN DIEGO MUSEUM OF MAN

PREFACE

Technology has had a profound effect on the evolution of human culture. Most recently, the "Information Technology" revolution ushered in by the computer chip, personal computer, and Internet have totally reorganized the way millions of people work, play, wage war, and interact the world over.[1] Archaeology provides a unique lens for examining a series of the most critical technological revolutions that have affected the rise and fall of societies and civilizations on the world scene from prehistoric to historic times. One of the most profound ancient technological revolutions concerns the discovery and adoption of metallurgy—the subject of *Journey to the Copper Age: Archaeology in the Holy Land*.

The prehistorian V. Gordon Childe referred to the adoption of agriculture and the domestication of animals around ten thousand years ago as the "Neolithic Revolution."[2] After more than 1.8 million years of hunting and gathering in the Middle East, humans could control food production through new agrotechnologies. Similarly, the technological changes brought about by the development of pyrotechnology—the intentional use and control of fire by humans—also played a crucial role in promoting social change. Around six thousand years ago, by being able to achieve higher and higher temperatures under controlled conditions, societies in the Middle East were able to bring about what I refer to as the "Metal Revolution."[3] For the first time, pyrotechnology enabled people to chemically reduce, or smelt, copper ore into metal. The metal was then cast into either prestige objects or tools, which were used to build social hierarchies and facilitate trade. Some of the earliest evidence of metal production has been discovered in the deserts of the Holy Land (the area including modern Israel, Palestine, Jordan, southern Lebanon, Syria, and the Sinai Peninsula). *Journey to the Copper Age* tells the fascinating story of this critical development in human history.

Journey to the Copper Age: Copper Ore, Donkeys, and the Desert

The discovery of the earliest metal production in the Holy Land has revealed the profound effect that it had on the evolution of Middle Eastern societies. Until the recent advent of the silicon computer chip, metal was the most important material for modern societies. Ironically, at the time of the *Journey to the Copper Age* exhibition the price of copper skyrocketed, serving as a reminder of the importance metal still holds today. The earliest evidence of metal production in the world comes from Israel and Jordan, dating to around 4500 to 3600 BCE, within the Chalcolithic period.

Journey to the Copper Age revolves around a National Geographic Society (NGS) expedition I was privileged to lead in 1997, when a group of international scientists joined me in riding donkeys across the deserts of Jordan and Israel to reconstruct the ancient trade route, mining methods, and ore smelting that were first used more than six thousand years ago. Joining me in conducting the expedition's main experiments were archaeometallurgist Professor Andreas Hauptmann of the German Mining Museum (GMM) in Bochum and archaeologist Dr. Mohammad Najjar from the Department of Antiquities of Jordan (DAJ).

Journey to the Copper Age is based primarily on excavations that I directed in Israel during the 1980s and 1990s, which were sponsored by the National Endowment for the Humanities (NEH), the NGS, and the C. Paul Johnson Family Foundation (in Napa, California, and Chicago).[4] To contextualize the "Metal Revolution" that took place more than six thousand years ago in the Holy Land, we also draw on excavations and fieldwork that I conducted in Jordan with Mohammad Najjar, Russell Adams, and other colleagues. Also exhibited and discussed in detail are metal masterpieces from the Chalcolithic metal hoard discovered in the "Cave of the Treasure" by Israeli archaeologist Psaach Bar Adon in the early 1960s. To date, these discoveries represent the earliest, most elaborate and sophisticated prehistoric metallurgical remains found in the world. How these objects and the technologies used to produce them functioned in Chalcolithic society provides a lens for helping researchers understand the role of technology in culture change during this formative period.

I am extremely grateful to the funding organizations for their long-term support of my research, and to my scholarly colleagues who have played a key role in exploring the impact of metal on ancient societies. The San Diego Museum of Man (SDMM) is very fortunate to have many of the artifacts found on our excavations, along with several from other expeditions on loan from the Israel Museum in Jerusalem. I am very grateful to Osnat Misch-Brandl, curator of the Chalcolithic and Bronze Age Antiquities in the Israel Museum, for her help and insight in creating the exhibit. To help contextualize the metal revolution, it is essential to understand what came before and after the Copper Age. Thus, we draw on artifacts from the Neolithic period (about 9000–4500 BCE), the Bronze Age (3600–2000 BCE), and through the Iron Age (about 1200–500 BCE). These artifacts were found on excavations that I conducted with Najjar and others in the rich copper ore district of Faynan in southern Jordan. As Faynan was one of the main Eastern Mediterranean source areas for copper ore from the Neolithic though the biblical periods (Bronze and Iron Ages), and up to Islamic times, it provides us with an integrated picture of the history of mining, metallurgy, trade, and society during these ancient times. Special thanks to the DAJ—especially Dr. Fawwaz al-Khraysheh, director general, and Dr. Ghazi Bisheh, former director general—for their strong support of archaeological work in Jordan that provides research institutions like the University of California, San Diego (UCSD), the opportunity to maintain study collections and other resources. Some of the artifacts in *Journey to the Copper Age* come from the collections of the UCSD Levantine Archaeology Laboratory, made possible through the permanent loan program of the DAJ.

The exhibition and this book are tied together by the NGS expedition in spring 1997, which brought together Israeli, Jordanian, German, and American researchers for the first time to carry out an experimental archaeology project concerning the earliest copper production in the Holy Land. I am grateful to the expedition team members, including Najjar, Hauptmann, Dr. Pierre Bikai, the late David Alon,

Dodik Shoshani, Izat Abu Rabia, Avner Goren, Kenneth Garrett, Elie Rogers, Chris Klein, and Katherine Ozment, who rode donkeys with me for ten days across the deserts of Jordan and Israel. Aspects of the research described here have been stimulated by my recent involvement with the Global Moments in Levant project of the University of Bergen, Norway, spearheaded by Leif Manger and Oystein LaBianca; and with the UCSD California Institute for Telecommunication and Information Technology (Calit2) under the direction of Professor Larry Smarr and UCSD Division Director Professor Ramesh Rao.

I am especially grateful to Adolfo Muniz, my colleague and former graduate student, for his creativity with the exhibition and help in organizing this book. I also extend warm thanks to David Mayo who designed the exhibition, Danny Brauer who designed this book, and Michelle Ghaffari who copy edited the manuscript. At the SDMM, I would particularly like to thank Executive Director Dr. Mari Lyn Salvador for her vision of bringing "town and gown" together, inviting me to be the guest curator of this exhibition, and for providing her unwavering support throughout this project. For their help with the exhibit, I thank Philip Hoog, curator of Archaeological Collections; Kathleen Hamilton, curator of Education and Interpretation; Angela Coleman, graphics artist; Javier Guerrero, director of operations; and Elle Vitte, PMP.

I would like to express my gratitude to the following friends and colleagues who provided illustrations, comments, excavation collaborations, scholarly critiques, and other help with the exhibition and book: Dr. Mohammad Najjar, the late David Alon, Professor Avraham Biran, Dr. Caroline Grigson, Dr. Yoav Arbel, Dr. Margie Burton, Professor Gary Rollefson, Dr. Yorke Rowan, Dr. Morag Kersel, Professor Yuval Goren, Dr. Edwin van den Brink, Ibrahim al-Assam, Hanni Hirsh, Rahamim Goren, Professor Symour Gitin, the late Omar Jibreen, and late Said Freij; Jean Perrot, Etienne Nodet, Dr. Catherine Commenge, the late Patti Rabbitt, Tom Ludovise, Juan Moreno, Dr. Jim Anderson, Dr. Jonathan Golden, Professor Ami Mazar, Dr. David Ilan, Dr. Daniella E. Bar-Yosef Mayer, Dr. Sarah Witcher-Kansa, Aladdin Madi, Marc Beherec, Kyle Knabb, Sarah Malena, Erez Ben-Yosef, Professor Lisa Tauxe, Professor Michael Homan, Professor Isaac Gilead, Professor Israel Finkelstein, Dr. Piotr Bienkowski, Dr. Eveline van der Steen, Dr. Steve Savage, Professor Larry Stager, Dr. Tom Higham, Professor Paul Goldberg, Dr. Francois Valla, the late Nadine Menahem, the late Professor Andrew Sherratt, Professor Patricia Smith, the late Professor Alan Witten, Professor Steve Rosen, Professor Arlene Rosen, Professor William G. Dever, Professor Mirek Barta, Dr. Stephen Bourke, Dr. Peta Seaton, Professor Sariel Shalev, and Dr. Hauptmann; Nadine Riedl, Vorderasiasiatisches Museum Berlin; Dorthea Arnold, Isabel Stuenkel and William Barrette of the Metropolitan Museum of Art, New York; Tibor Toth, Toth Graphix; and at the NGS for their generosity and help: Dr. John Francis, Susan Norton, Billie Leff, Wendy Glassmire, and Chris Klein. A special thanks to the American Center of Oriental Research (ACOR) in Amman, Jordan, and its former

Director Dr. Pierre Bikai, former Associate Director Dr. Patricia Bikai, Director Dr. Barbara A. Porter, and staff members: Christopher A. Tuttle, Kathy Nimri, Nisreen Abu al-Shaikh, Mohammad Adawi, Sa'id Adawi, and Abed Adwi, for their help with my fieldwork in Jordan. I am indebted to my India ethnoarchaeology project colleagues: Alina Levy, D. Radhakrishna Sthapathy, D. Srikanda Sthapathy, and D. Swaminatha Sthapathy for their contributions, and P. Prakash Jaising for introducing me to the hereditary bronze casters of Swamimalai. Thanks also to the Sterling Swamimalai Heritage Hotel for their fine hospitality.

I would also like to thank my colleagues in the UCSD Judaic Studies Program for their long-time support: Professors David Goodblatt, William Propp, David Noel Freedman, Deborah Hertz, and Richard Elliott Friedman (Emeritus), Janice Dempsey, Erin Svalstad, and Dorothy Wagoner. In the Department of Anthropology, thanks to the late Professor Don Tuzin; and Professors Joel Robbins, Guillermo Algaze, Geoff Braswell, Paul Goldstein, Robert McC. Adams, and Margaret Schoeninger. I am grateful for the collaboration and support of my colleagues at Calit2 on this project: Rao, Doug Ramsey (a superb filmmaker who is responsible for producing our ethnoarchaeology film that accompanies the SDMM exhibition), Alexander Matthews, Laura Wolzon, and Srinivas Sukumar. The fieldwork and logistics described here would not have been possible without the help of UCSD administrators, including Chancellor Mary Anne Fox, Senior Vice Chancellor of Academic Affairs Marsha Chandler, Social Science Dean Paul Drake, Vice Chancellor for Research and Dean of Graduate Studies Richard Attiyeh, Resource Administration Director Helen Szkorla, Associate Vice Chancellor David Miller, and University Librarian Dr. Brian Schottlaender. A special personal thanks to the Viterbi Family Foundation and Dr. Uri Hersher, founding president and chief executive officer of the Skirball Cultural Center, for their early support of this exhibition, and C. Paul Johnson for his long-term support of my archaeological research in Israel and Jordan. A special thanks to Norma and Rueben Kershaw for their strong support of all my research endeavors. I would also like to thank my sons, Ben and Gil, for putting up with so many of my absences from home while they were growing up and hope they will reflect on the good times we had in the deserts of Israel and Jordan when they were able to join me. Finally, I am especially happy to dedicate this book to my wife, Alina, who has accompanied me on this journey from its inception along the banks of the Wadi Beersheva almost thirty years ago.

Thomas E. Levy

CHAPTER ONE

THE METAL REVOLUTION IN THE HOLY LAND

Imagine a world without metal. Today, our lives are intertwined with the use of metal for everything from cars, computer chips, and dental fillings to the buildings we live in and the tools we use to help us interact with the world around us. Now consider the time when the earliest hominids, *Homo erectus*, left Africa and reached the land bridge connecting that continent with Asia—between 1.8 and 1 million years ago. The countries that make up that land bridge today include Israel, the Palestinian National Authority (PNA), Jordan, Egypt's Sinai Peninsula, Lebanon, and southern Syria (figs. 1.2, 1.3). This region is referred to as the Holy Land, because so much fundamental history of the Jewish, Christian, and Moslem peoples took place there. It is along this sacred land bridge that human groups lived as small-scale hunting, gathering, and foraging societies for almost 1.8 million years, until the advent of the Neolithic period and the domestication of plants and animals around eight to eleven thousand years ago. For the first time, humans became food producers—able to provide their own crops and animals—so that they could supply sustenance to an ever-increasing population. This is why archaeologists refer to this radical new change in subsistence as the "Neolithic Revolution."

FIGURE 1.1

UCSD archaeologist Tom Levy mines malachite copper ore in the Wadi Khalid, Faynan district, Jordan, as part of a National Geographic Society-sponsored expedition in March 1997. The donkeys seen in the background were used to transport the ore to the border of Israel, where they were exchanged for "Israeli" donkeys.

Photograph by Kenneth Garrett, National Geographic.

FIGURE 1.2 (OVERLEAF)

The timeline chronologically traces the beginnings of mining and metal production in the Holy Land from the Neolithic period through biblical times in the Iron Age. The Chalcolithic period can be seen in relation to ancient world cultural, pre-historic, and historic events.

HOLY LAND TIMELINE 9000–586 BCE

| Pre-Pottery Neolithic ca. 10,000–5500 BCE | Pottery Neolithic ca. 55000–4500 BCE | Chalcolithic Period ca. 4500–3600 BCE |

Holy Land Settlements

4300 BCE
Ghassul C–A
Golan 12 Peqi'in
Nahal Qanah
  (Gold Deposit)
Cave of the Warrior
Abu Hof
Shiqmim 3–2

3600 BCE
Givat HaOranim
Gilat (two "late" dates)
Lower Egypt Sites:
Maadi
Buto

7500–6000 BCE
Ain Ghazal
Basta
Jericho
Gwair
Tel Tif'dan
Nahal Hemar

5500 BCE
Munhata 2a
Wadi Rabah
Ain el-Jarba
Teleilat Ghassul H–J
Tel Tsaf I
Jericho VIII
Abu Hamid (Lower)

| 9000 | 7500 | 6000 | 4500 | 4300 | 4000 | 3600 |

6000 BCE
Jericho IX
Ziglab 200
Nahal Qanah
  (Neolithic Deposit)
Munhata
Nizzanim

4800 BCE
Jericho VIII
Abu Hamid (Lower)
Kfar Samir Uvda
Megadim
Beth Shean XVIII
Wadi Rabah
Gilat IV

4500 BCE
Ghassul D–G
Golan 18
Beth Shean XVII
Grar
Gilat IIIA–B
Besor Sites:
Qatif Y–3
Peqi'in, Shiqmim 3–4

4000 BCE
Shiqmim 1–2
Beer Sheva Sites:
Abu Matar/Bir es-Safadi
Horvat Beter
Cave of the Treasure
Gilat IIA–B

3600 BCE
Halif Terrace IIIC
Wadi Fidan 4
Magass
Tour Ikhbeineh
Ashkelon Afridar

Contemporary World Events

ca. 8000–7500 Domesticated grains in Israel,
                Palestine, Jordan
ca. 7500 Copper ore used for beads and pigment in Jordan
ca. 7000–6000 Native copper used at Neolithic Catal
                Huyuk, Turkey
ca. 7000–5000 Small agricultural villages in China
ca. 7000–4500 Earliest permanent settlements in Egypt

ca. 4500 Mesopotamians build boats
ca. 4500 Cotton is cultivated in Mexico
ca. 4500–4000 Earliest temples in the Holy Land
ca. 4500–3500 Horses domesticated in region of Kazakhstan
ca. 4200–4000 Copper alloys used in the Holy Land
ca. 4000 Rice is grown as a food crop in China
ca. 4000–1800 Early ceramic cultures in Peru
ca. 3500–3000 Potters wheel used in Mesopotamia
ca. 3500–3000 Wheeled vehicles used in Sumer
ca. 3500–3000 Temples of Uruk in Mesopotamia
ca. 3300–1700 Indus Valley Civilization
ca. 3200 Sumerians use cuneiform writing on clay tablets
ca. 3200 Hieroglyphic writing appears in Egypt
ca. 3000 Construction on Stonehenge begins
ca. 3000 Evidence of settlements in Great Lakes Region

Early Bronze Age ca. 3600–2000 BCE	Middle Bronze Age ca. 2000–1600 BCE	Late Bronze Age ca. 1600–1200 BCE	Iron Age I ca. 1200–1000 BCE	Iron Age II ca. 1000–586 BCE

3300 BCE	**2000 BCE**	**1550 BCE**	**1200–1140/30 BCE**	**1000/980–840/830 BCE**	**732/701–605/586 BCE**
Halif Terrace IIIA-B	Tel Dan	Tell es-Sa'idieh	Khirbat en-Nahas SIV	Khirbat en-Nahas AIII/IIB	Busayra
Lachish (NW)	Tell el-Hayyat	Deir Alla	Ashkelon	Gezer IX-VIII	Tel Jemmeh "AB"
Tel Erani Str. D/C-Str. V	Pella	Rehov	Ekron VII	Rehov VI-IV	Megiddo III
Tel Arad IV	Megiddo	Beth Shean	Ashdod XIIIb	Megiddo VB-IVB/VA	Hazor IV-III
En Besor III	Tell el-Ajjul	Megiddo	Ebal	Hazor Xb-VIII	Arad VII-VI
	Tel Michal	Deir el-Balah	Tell es-Sa'idiyeh cemetery	Ekron IV	Tell el-Kheleifeh III-IV
	Beth Shean	Shiqmona	Raddana	Arad XII	Rehov II
	Gezer	Aphek	Izbet Sartah III	Tell el-Kheleifeh Period I	
	Hazor	Lachish	Megiddo VIIA		
		Timna 23, 15, 185	Dan VI		
			Hazor XII		

```
  3000      2500      2000      1500      1200  1100      1000      900      800      700      600
```

3000–2300 BCE	**2300 BCE**	**1140/30–1000/980 BCE**	**840/830–732/701 BCE**
Arad III-II	Khirbat Hamra Ifdan II	Khirbat en-Nahas SIV	Khirbat en-Nahas AIIB
Megiddo XVII-XV	Bab edh-Dhra	Wadi Fidan 40 cemetery	Gezer VII-VI
Beth Shean XII-XI	Beer Resisim	Ekron VI-IV	Hazor VII-Va
Khirbat Hamra Ifdan IIIA-B	En Ziq	Ashdod XIIIa-XI	Megiddo IVA
Barqa el-Hetiye	Jebel Qa'aqir	Dan Vb-Va	Rehov III
Yarmuth Area A4-7	Khirbat Iskander	Megiddo VIB-VIA	Arad XI-VIII
Tel Halif XIII-XI	Timna 149	Hazor XI	Tell el-Kheleifeh II
			Timna 30
			Faynan 7

ca. 2650   Great pyramid of Giza
ca. 2600   Sphinx
ca. 2600   Chinese begin cultivating silkworms
ca. 2500   Egyptians discover use of papyrus
ca. 2100   Ziggurat at Ur
ca. 2000–1500   Babylonians use highly developed geometry
ca. 1800   Palace of Knossos built in Crete
ca. 1800   Rise of Germanic Tribes
ca. 1800–1500   Pre-Olmec cultures
ca. 1750   Code of Hammurabi
ca. 1600   Mound complexes built in Mississippi Valley
ca. 1400–400   Olmec cultures in Mesoamerica
ca. 1300–1200   Trojan War

ca. 1287   Battle of Kadesh led by Rameses the Great
ca. 1250   Lion gate built at Mycenae
ca. 1206   Israel mentioned on Merneptah Stele
ca. 1200   Collapse of Late Bronze Age Civilizations in Eastern Mediterranean and Israelite settlement in Holy Land
ca. 1100   First large New World sculpture (Olmec, Tenochtitlan, Mexico)
ca. 1000   David conquers Jerusalem
ca. 1000   Emergence of Adena culture along the Ohio River
ca. 922   Divided monarchy of Israel and Judea
ca. 900   Chavin cultures in Peru
ca. 800   Homer's *Iliad* and *Odyssey* written
ca. 776   First Olympic games in Greece
ca. 743   Messinian Wars
ca. 700   First writing in New World (Zapotec, San José Mogote, Mexico)
ca. 650–500   Hebrew Bible (Old Testament) written
ca. 600   First large stone pyramids in New World (Maya, Nakbe, Guatemala)
ca. 586   Babylonian destruction of the Temple in Jerusalem

Peqi'in •

Golan Heights

• Rasm Harbush

■ **Haifa**

Sea of Galilee

Nablus
■

Mediterranean Sea

• Nahal Qanah

• Abu Hamid

Tel Aviv
■ • Azor

Amman
▲ ■

• Ben Shemen

• Ain Ghazal

Palmahim •

• Cave of the Warrior

Jerusalem ■

• Tuleilat Ghassul

Jericho • ▲

En Gedi •

Dead Sea

• Grar

Cave of the Treasure •

Kissufim •

• Gilat

Beersheva

• Tel Arad

Shiqmim • ■

Abu Matar

Horvat Beter

Bir es-Safadi

Tel Tif'dan ▲

Faynan Copper

• Ghwair

• Ba'ja

Timna Copper •

Ein Umm Ahmad •

Serabit el-Khadem • *Copper*

Ein Huderah •

■ Modern Cities
• Chalcolithic Sites
▲ Neolithic Sites

50 Kilometers

31 Miles

Red Sea

Shortly after the Neolithic Revolution, another fundamental change took place between six to seven thousand years ago, which I refer to as the "Metal Revolution." As the world's earliest *technological* revolution, the development of ancient metallurgy helped to change the character of societies from the egalitarian type typical of the small hunting and gathering bands that characterized some 1.8 million years of prehistory in the Holy Land, to much larger scale and complex social organizations know as chiefdoms, where status and rank were inherited for the first time. In egalitarian societies one had to earn social position by being an excellent hunter, gather, forager, and so on. With the rise of chiefdoms, social positions were inherited—if you were born as the offspring of a chief, you inherited a social position of power and prestige. One of the reasons the rise of chiefdoms fascinates anthropologists is because once this social organization "threshold" was crossed, there was no going back to egalitarian ways of life. The seeds of our basic social structure were sown with the emergence of chiefdoms. One region that provides the earliest evidence of this kind of social evolution is the Holy Land, which is also known as the southern Levant. With the discovery and adoption of metallurgy, some of the early chiefdoms of the southern Levant used this technology to strengthen their social and economic position. The following are some of the questions addressed in *Journey to the Copper Age*: Why was early metallurgy so important to this radical new form of social organization that ushered in institutionalized social inequality? How was early metallurgy carried out? Who actually controlled the production of the earliest metals in the Holy Land? What is it about ancient and traditional metallurgy that infused it with not only economic importance but with highly charged ritual and religious dimensions (figs. 1.1, 1.4)? Equally important, what other new social and economic developments took place when metallurgy first emerged?

Pyrotechnology and Social Change

The discovery of metallurgy and the production of other synthetic materials represented a groundbreaking change in the way peoples could manipulate their natural environments. Prior to the Neolithic period, for well over one million years, humans used "unaltered" materials such as stone, wood, bone, antler, shell, and leather to make tools. When ancient humans discovered the ability to change matter from one state to another, profound transformations occurred not only in their ability to manipulate the world around them but also in their spiritual behavior. In *The Forge and the Crucible: The Origins and Structures of Alchemy*, Mircea Eliade, the distinguished University of Chicago professor of the history of religion, shows how people's awareness of the astonishing new power of metallurgy led to deep changes in belief systems and ritual.[5] The power of transforming ore into metal and the production of objects in traditional societies can be observed amongst contemporary cultures in Africa and India. By carrying out ethnoarchaeological research of these traditional metal workers, it is possible to understand how metallurgy was

FIGURE 1.3

Map of the southern Levant, or Holy Land, with selected Neolithic and Chalcolithic sites. The Holy Land comprises present-day Israel, the Palestine National Authority, Jordan, Lebanon, Syria, and the Sinai Peninsula.

Map by Adolfo Muniz and Thomas Levy; relief by Tibor Toth, Toth Graphix.

FIGURE 1.4

The team rides through the deep canyon of the Wadi Dana in the copper-ore-rich Faynan district of Jordan. Although the expedition lasted ten days, two days were lost in negotiations with local officials to gain permission to travel into different territories. Similar problems would have affected ancient caravans.

Photograph by Kenneth Garrett, National Geographic.

carried out in antiquity and how it may have functioned in social and religious domains of ancient peoples. The relationship between these modern studies of traditional metal work and the Chalcolithic crafts people in the southern Levant are explored toward the end of *Journey to the Copper Age*.

In essence, pyrotechnology is the intentional use of fire and its control by human beings. While possible evidence for the use of fire for cooking may occur as early as 1.5 million years ago in Swartskrans Cave, South Africa, more widespread evidence for cooking is found in Middle Paleolithic (about 80 to 250 thousand years ago), in Israel and other regions. Perhaps the first marked shift from using fire for cooking and forcing game animals across hunting landscapes occurred at the same time as the Neolithic Revolution when, in the Middle Eastern oases of Jericho and other locales, special clay ovens (*tabun* in Arabic) were used to bake bread. As archaeologist Colin Renfrew suggests, one can hypothesize that early experiments in pyrotechnology based on ovens may have led to the discovery of firing clay and, ultimately, to the firing of pottery in primitive kilns.[6] While the earliest pottery was baked hard in open fires, "reducing" conditions (removing oxygen) could be reached in clay ovens, or kilns, by limiting the flow of air and adding charcoal. Firing pottery in a reduced atmosphere resulted in a much stronger and useful end product. By becoming "Masters of Fire," using Eliade's term, the foundations were laid for reaching temperatures as high as $1,083°$C $(1,891°$F$)$, the amount of heat needed to smelt copper ore into metal.

Obviously, these technological changes related to pyrotechnology did not occur overnight or on one particular day. It is impossible to pinpoint a specific date or even cluster of years when metal production first appeared; therefore, is it justifiable to use the term *revolution* to describe the appearance of metal and metal production in the archaeological record? To help explain the concept of rapid change in the archaeological record, Stephen Jay Gould and Niles Eldredge's concept of "Punctuated equilibrium" is extremely useful.[7] Accordingly, the main idea is that changes in species is represented as a kind of gradual Darwinian evolution, except that it is "punctuated" by periods of rapid evolutionary changes. This model works well for conceptualizing the Metal Revolution, in which fire played a critical role in human subsistence for over one million years, then "suddenly," during Neolithic and Chalcolithic period, experiments with pyrotechnology led first to the production of pottery and second to the production of metal.

CHAPTER TWO

BEFORE THE METAL REVOLUTION
THE NEOLITHIC PERIOD

Life during the Neolithic Period

To understand the significance of the appearance of metal production in the archaeological record of the Middle East, it is important to understand some of the social and economic developments that were in place on the eve of the Metal Revolution. The period that precedes the Copper Age, or Chalcolithic period, is known as the Neolithic period. In the southern Levant, the Neolithic period (about 8500–4500 BCE) was also a time of great innovation. During this time, many pre-historic societies made the transition from hunting, gathering, and foraging to agriculture, resulting in what is called the "Neolithic Revolution." The domestication of crops and animals helped initiate the beginning of permanent farming villages in the Middle East in the "Fertile Crescent," the region where over one hundred Neolithic sites have been scientifically excavated. The Fertile Crescent represents a broad arch of grasslands and open oak and pistachio woodlands, which spans over 2,000 kilometers, beginning in the Negev desert of Israel and extending north into Lebanon, Turkey, and across the Zagros Mountains through Iraq and Iran. This region contained the wild progenitors of both the animals and plants that became the main domesticates used by the early Neolithic farmers and are still used today. These include wild sheep, goats, pigs, and cattle; and the wild ancestors of einkorn wheat (*Triticum monococcum*) and barley (*Hordeum vulgare*). The domestication of plants and animals enabled societies to shift from being dependent on nonreliable wild food resources to becoming independent food producers. Surplus food supplies during the Neolithic created opportunities for occupations that went beyond subsistence needs. Some of these new developments included moderate increases in human population density, long-distance trade in obsidian (volcanic glass suitable for making stone tools), changes in belief systems, the initiation of rectilinear building technology to accommodate the growing village populations, and craft production.

FIGURE 2.1

Aerial view of Tel Tif'dan, a PPN site situated at the "gateway" to the Faynan copper ore district in Jordan.

Helicopter courtesy of Her Majesty Queen Noor of Jordan and the Royal Jordanian Air Force.

Photograph by Thomas Levy, UCSD Levantine Archaeology Laboratory.

FIGURE 2.2

Plastered anthropomorphic
statues from the Pre-Pottery
Neolithic (PPN) site of Ain
Ghazal, Jordan.

Photograph courtesy of Gary Rollefson.

Time Line of Technology in the Southern Levant—Neolithic Roots

To understand the magnitude of change that the Chalcolithic metal revolution
represents, it is useful to conceptualize how traditional technologies developed.
The oldest technologies are based on the use of unaltered materials such as wood,
leather, stone, flint (chert), bone, antler, and shell. In the Holy Land, technological
change took place over hundreds of thousands of years, and only in the Pre-Pottery
Neolithic (PPN) period, approximately 8500 BCE, did people begin to employ heat,
or pyrotechnology, to alter matter and create synthetic materials such as lime plaster. By the end of the Neolithic period, around 6000 BCE, pottery making was first
discovered, enabling people to cook and store foodstuffs in clay vessels. Some of the
most spectacular PPN sites have been found at Jericho in the PNA,[8] and at numerous
locales in Jordan, such as Ain Ghazal,[9] Ba'ja near Petra,[10] Ghwair,[11] and Tel Tif'dan,
near the gateway to the copper ore district of Faynan.[12]

Ain Ghazal Statues and Faynan Ore

Symbolic artifacts, such as statuary and figurines, provide a window on the cognitive belief systems and rituals that played a critical role in ancient societies. Neolithic sites in the southern Levant have produced some of the most spectacular ancient prehistoric art in the world. In excavations at the extensive PPN site of Ain Ghazal near Amman, in the present-day capital of Jordan, archaeologist Gary Rollefson discovered more than thirty stunning statues ranging from small portrait busts to large life-size figures (fig. 2.2). Artisans of the Neolithic period constructed each statue using a reed frame, which was covered with a mixture of clay and burnt limestone plaster. The production of plaster involved significant mastery of pyro-technology and marks the beginning of the road to pottery manufacture and metal production. PPN settlements are characterized by the widespread use of plaster for floors, stone and mudbrick walls, two-story houses, courtyards, and other features.[13] Studies of trace elements show that the artisans of Ain Ghazal used copper ore from the Faynan district, located over 200 kilometers away, to paint lifelike eyes on the statues. The beginnings of long-distance trade and the development of a PPN interaction sphere for exchange was a hallmark of this period.[14] As each face is different on these statues, and those found at other Neolithic sites, researchers generally agree that these objects were used in an ancestor cult of some kind that focused on individual families.

Settlements during the PPN period were characterized primarily by autonomous village sites. The site of Tel Tif'dan (around 7500 BCE), excavated by combined efforts of the team of UCSD, Department of Antiquities of Jordan (DAJ), and University of Bristol (England) archaeologists, is an example of a typical PPN village (fig. 2.1). It is located at the mouth of the Wadi Fidan, the gateway to the copper district of Faynan in southern Jordan. The site sits on the eastern edge of the Arabah (in Arabic)/Arava (in Hebrew) valley like a lone sentinel on a small, isolated mesa top approximately 0.05 hectares (0.12 acres) in area; as such, it is naturally defended. The preservation of the village architecture at Tel Tif'dan is remarkable, with many of the walls preserved to a height of over 2 meters (about 6.5 feet). Inside the rooms of this prehistoric village, a wealth of artifacts were discovered including figurines, animal bones, flint tools, ground stone tools, and other objects.

Excavations at Tel Tif'dan revealed thousands of locally produced artifacts. Many of the rooms excavated at the site contained large numbers of flint drills and bead blanks, indicating the presence of a bead industry. To understand how some of these tools may have been used, archaeologists rely on ancient historical sources, experimental archaeology, and ethnoarchaeology. Ethnoarchaeology refers to the study of contemporary cultures with the aim of understanding the relationship between behavior and material culture. As such, by studying traditional cultures such as modern hunter-gatherers, pastoral nomads, and village peoples, it is possible for archaeologists to build analogical models about the way in which people interacted with their material culture to help explain the dynamics of ancient

FIGURE 2.3

Stone PPN drills made of flint
from Tel Tif'dan were used in
the local production of beads.
Thousands of drills and piercing
tools were found at this site in
the Faynan district, dating to
around 7500 BCE. The production of large quantities of beads
from Tel Tif'dan probably
contributed to its inclusion in
the "PPN Interaction Sphere."

Photograph by Tim Stahl, San Diego
Museum of Man.

FIGURE 2.4

Wall painting of Egyptian
workers using a bow drill from
Theban Tomb 100 (the Tomb
of Rekh-mi-Re at). The tomb is
located in Qurna on the western bank of Thebes, Egypt. New
Kingdom, Eighteenth Dynasty,
approximately 1550–1295 BCE.
Wall paintings such as this and
other historical documents help
archaeologists reconstruct how
prehistoric technologies may
have worked.

Rogers Fund, 1935 (35.101.1).
Facsimile copy by Nina de Garis Davies.
Photograph courtesy of the Metropolitan
Museum of Art, New York.

24

FIGURE 2.5

Like the ancient Egyptian
carpenters using a bow drill,
these two carpenters working
in the village of Swamimalai,
Tamil Nadu, India, use a thin
piece of rope to power the drill.
One of the men holds the drill
while the other uses a string
to spin it. Ethnoarchaeological
observations such as this help
archaeologists understand
ancient technologies.

*Photograph by Thomas Levy, UCSD
Levantine Archaeology Laboratory.*

cultures encountered in the archaeological record. For example, during the course
of an ethnoarchaeological study carried out recently in a small village in the Indian
state of Tamil Nadu, several carpenters used a type of drill depicted on ancient
Egyptian wall reliefs dating to more than 3,500 years ago. Seeing is believing, and
having had the opportunity to record exactly how a string- or rope-powered drill
works today provides a remarkable model for how Neolithic "drillers" used their
flint drill bits more than nine thousand years ago (figs. 2.3–2.5).

Tel Tif'dan dates to the end of the PPN period and has a number of fascinating
features that link it to the greater world of early farming societies spread across the
southern Levant. These elements include its location at the entrance to the Faynan
copper ore district, the discovery of a remarkable amount of specialized drilling
tools used for making beads, the beautifully preserved architecture, and the large
number of small clay figurines representing human and animal forms. Even during
this formative period of social change, therefore, people were drawn to the Faynan
region by its beauty and the importance of raw copper ore for crafting ornaments.

CHAPTER THREE

THE CHALCOLITHIC PERIOD
LIFE DURING THE METAL REVOLUTION

The Metal Revolution did not occur in a vacuum. During the Chalcolithic period, a "package" of fundamental new social and economic developments occurred. *Journey to the Copper Age* takes us not only to the most visible of those changes— the emergence of metal production—but also to a landscape filled with new settlement systems, people with more sophisticated methods of farming and herding than their Neolithic predecessors, more complex religious institutions, and a host of other changes. Anthropological archaeology provides us with the theories, methods, and data needed to explain how and why these changes took place.

The Holy Land has been witness to a number of population explosions over the past six thousand years. The first dramatic increase in human population occurred during the Chalcolithic period (4500–3600 BCE), beginning around 4500 BCE. It is against this background of population increase that archaeologists have been able to document a corresponding increase in social complexity and the emergence of a new type of society—primarily chiefdoms. The Chalcolithic (in Greek, *Chalco* translates to copper and *lithic* to stone) period gave rise to new ideas and innovations ranging from advanced settlements, social organization, and crafts production to religious beliefs and burial practices. The inhabitants relied less on hunting than their predecessors in earlier periods and developed new methods of more intensively exploiting the milk, wool, hair, and traction of domestic animals such as sheep, goats, and cattle. Like their Neolithic ancestors, they cultivated wheat, barley, and lentils; however, some of the earliest evidence of flood-water farming— a primitive kind of irrigation technology—exists from the Chalcolithic period. Horticulture, the growing of garden plants, also developed during the Copper Age when dates and olives were first extensively cultivated. It is within this constellation of new developments in population growth, agrotechnology, innovative settlement systems, and other changes that the emergence of metal production is viewed.[15]

The Paleoenvironmental Context

Many of the most impressive Copper Age settlements in the southern Levant, such as Shiqmim, Gilat, Tuleilat Ghassul, and the Judean desert cave sites, are located in austere and inhospitable desert environments (fig. 3.2). Archaeologists use a wide range of sources to reconstruct the ancient environment of the Middle East. Just as the modern world is experiencing climate change due to global warming and other factors, there have also been fluctuations in climate over the past ten thousand years. Although many people think of deserts as static environments

FIGURE 3.1

A portion of the more than four hundred copper objects dating from the late fifth millennium BCE, which were found in the Cave of the Treasure. The site is located in the Judean desert of Israel. Shown here are copper mace heads, scepters, crowns, and other objects. Note the elaborate twin-headed ibex mace head in the lower right. Most of these metal works were made with the lost wax method of casting. Experimental archaeology in south India successfully replicated this particular mace head.

Photograph by Kenneth Garrett, National Geographic.

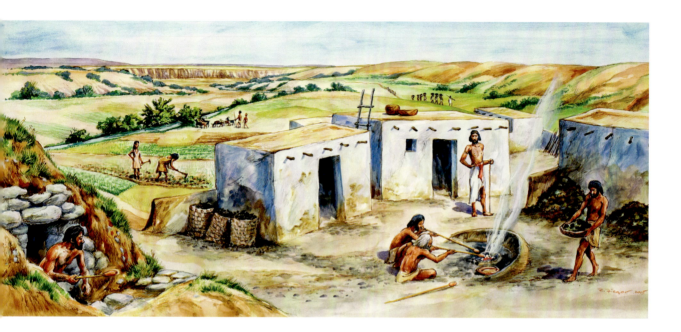

FIGURE 3.2

An artist's reconstruction of smelting activities carried out at the Shiqmim Chalcolithic village. Sacks of charcoal can be seen lying against a rectilinear building in the prehistoric village. The man on the left emerges from a subterranean room with a blow pipe coated with a clay tip.

Artwork by Reiner Zieger, Berlin.

due to geomorphological processes today and ancient environmental processes in the past, it cannot be assumed that the climate of the past was similar to what we experience in the twenty-first century. Environmental scientists help archaeologists piece together the character of the ancient environment, and a variety of sources have demonstrated that the climate at the beginning of the Chalcolithic period was about 100 millimeters wetter than the climate of today. The environment grew increasingly drier after around 3600 BCE.

To identify changing environments through time, researchers study a variety of data including paleolimnology, or the fluctuations in ancient lakes such as the Dead Sea,[16] the shifting distribution of fossil land snails for evidence of what type of vegetation they ate (Mediterranean versus desert plants),[17] changes in tree pollen to identify the presence or absence of tree cover in a region,[18] and geomorphology.[19] After some thirty years of science-based paleoenvironmental studies in the southern Levant, a picture has emerged that at the beginning of the Chalcolithic period, around 4500 BCE, the environment was considerably wetter, with around 100 millimeters more average annual rainfall. If we consider that successful dry-farming requires approximately 200 to 250 millimeters of average annual rainfall, the main Chalcolithic village settlements in the northern Negev desert (Wadi Beersheva) fall well below today's 200-millmeter rainfall zone. Given the paleoenvironmental data, however, we can now add 100 millimeters of average annual rainfall to this distribution, meaning there was well over 300 millimeters of rainfall available for crops with dry-farming methods. As seen in the reconstruction of the Beersheva valley during the Chalolithic period, paleoenvironmental and archaeological data suggest that there was a perennial stream in the valley at this time, which was used for

simple irrigation farming. By adding irrigation water to the equation, the farmers of the Chalcolithic period could effectively create their own moist Mediterranean climate conditions in the valley bottoms of the desert.

The Search for the Dead Sea Scrolls and the Accidental Discovery of the Cave of the Treasure

Recognition of the Metal Revolution in the southern Levant is encapsulated in the discovery of a remarkable hoard of Chalcolithic copper metal objects found in a remote cave in the Judean desert. The discovery of the Dead Sea Scrolls in the late 1940s encouraged archaeologists from the newly established state of Israel to search for more scrolls around the western shores of the Dead Sea beginning in 1960. This led to the remarkable unearthing of the now-famous Chalcolithic metal hoard in the "Cave of the Treasure" in 1961 (fig. 3.1). Following Israeli archaeologist Psaach Bar Adon's discovery of this treasure trove, researchers are still challenged by the sophisticated methods used to produce the objects in the hoard. They continue to debate how these exquisite objects were made, the function they served, and the role they played in formative late fifth to fourth millennium societies in the Holy Land.[20] The black-and-white photographs shown here of the Cave of the Treasure were taken by renowned Israeli photographers, Rolf Kneller and Werner Braun, and recount Bar Adon's historic discovery.

Excavations over the past twenty years, experimental archaeology, and ethnoarchaeological research have provided a dynamic picture of how Chalcolithic societies in this part of the ancient Near East were organized and the importance of the beginnings of copper production for them (figs. 3.3–3.9).

FIGURE 3.3

Living in pup tents under difficult conditions, Bar Adon's expedition camp of 1960–61 was situated on the edge of the Nahal Mishmar in the Judean desert. The expedition was organized by Israeli researchers trying to locate more of the famous Dead Sea Scrolls.

Photograph by Rolf M. Kneller.

FIGURE 3.4

This expedition to the Judean desert took place under the direction of Israel's most distinguished archaeologists—Professors Yigael Yadin, Yohanan Aharoni, and Nahum Avigad. Psaach Bar Adon was given the responsibility of surveying the Nahal Mishmar. Late at night at the beginning of the expedition, Bar Adon (right) confers with Yadin (with pipe) in a tent, while Israel Defense Force (IDF) Brigadier General Avraham Yaffe of the Southern Command looks on.

Photograph by Rolf M. Kneller.

FIGURE 3.5

View of the Nahal Mishmar, Judean Desert. The opening to the cave is located in the cliff below. The IDF was ordered to provide manpower and facilities to assist in the survey of the arid valleys between Ein Gedi and Masada, located on the west coast of the Dead Sea.

Photograph by Rolf M. Kneller.

FIGURE 3.6

IDF soldiers help archaeologists assemble a rope ladder used to access the cave during the expedition.

Photograph by Rolf M. Kneller.

FIGURE 3.7

Bar Adon (with pipe) can be seen silhouetted at the mouth of the Cave of the Treasure, overlooking the Nahal Mishmar.

Photograph by Rolf M. Kneller.

FIGURE 3.8

Soldiers remove one of the large boulders that hindered access to the area where the copper hoard was located. By levering the stone to the cave entrance, it could be pushed off the precipice to fall more than 100 meters to the valley floor, thus opening the back of the cave to exploration.

Photograph by Werner Braun.

FIGURE 3.9

In April 1961 Bar Adon's team discovered the copper hoard. Bar Adon is shown here registering the finds at the time of discovery and the excitement of the moment is reflected in his excavation report:

At 2 P.M. on the eighth day of our work in the cave, one of the students, Ruth Pecherski, and one of the soldiers, Freddy Halperin, came upon the top of a sloping stone covering a natural niche in the northern wall of chamber B. This covering stone was flawed at the edges, so that at the very first glance several metal objects could be seen glinting through the cracks. We at once set about clearing away the loose earth all round the stone, until the whole of it was exposed. Then darkness forced us to stop working for the night. Early the next morning we started to lay bare the hoard…. It took us three hours to remove the articles, which were wrapped in a straw mat, from their hiding-place—four hundred and twenty eight in all. Apart from six hematite, six ivory and one stone, all the rest are of metal. They were all of a surprisingly high technical standard of workmanship.

(Psaach Bar Adon, "Expedition C: The Cave of the Treasure," *Israel Exploration Journal* 12 [1962]: 213-26.)

Photograph by Werner Braun.

A Revolution in Craft Specialization

While embryonic craft specialization was initiated during the Neolithic period, it was accompanied by much more complex levels of organization and diversification in the Chalcolithic period that followed. For example, the potter's wheel was invented, which enabled the mass production of pottery vessels.[21] There was also specialization in basalt bowl production and other stone objects,[22] ivory carving, bead manufacturing,[23] and, most significant, metallurgy. The earliest and most spectacular prehistoric metallurgical remains in the Middle East, and perhaps in the world, are represented by the famous Cave of the Treasure copper hoard. The collection includes over four hundred "prestige" copper objects, including crowns, scepters, mace heads, and other objects, most of which were made from copper metal by artisans employing the complex lost wax technique of metal casting. Composed of alloyed copper with relatively high percentages of antimony and arsenic, the prestige metal objects in the cache contain an alloyed copper that is not native to the Holy Land. Lead isotope, chemical, and other tests show that the alloyed copper for these objects probably originated over 1,000 kilometers from the southern Levant, somewhere in eastern Turkey and/or Azerbaijan in the Fertile Crescent.

FIGURE 3.10

A Chalcolithic metal masterpiece, this highly unusual mace head, topped by a mythological twin-headed ibex, was found in the Cave of the Treasure. Ibex still roam wild in the Judean desert, especially around the Ein Gedi spring. UCSD archaeologists worked closely with hereditary bronze casters in south India on an experimental archaeology project to re-create the lost wax method used to produce this tour de force.

Copper. Height 11 cm, length 14.3 cm, diameter 3.5 cm, weight 335 gr. IAA 1961-119.

Photograph courtesy of Israel Museum.

How and why these exquisite artifacts made from nonlocal metal came to be hidden in a cave in Israel is a major puzzle for archaeologists to this day.

When the Cave of the Treasure hoard was first found, archaeologists thought the objects—and lost wax casting—were too advanced for the local Chalcolithic peoples. Consequently, a model of diffusion was suggested whereby the exquisite metal hoard was thought to have originated in the Anatolia and the Caucasus, over 1,000 kilometers from Israel, where alloyed copper (including arsenic) is found. Researchers still have no clear idea where the actual source of the alloyed copper used in Chalcolithic prestige metal work came from or the precise methodology associated with the ancient lost wax technology (see note 20). There is agreement, however, that the production of prestige objects such as standards, crowns, and mace heads using alloyed copper was a specialized activity aimed at producing objects of high social value.

Three revolutionary developments in pyrotechnology contributed to the emergence and consolidation of social inequality in the southern Levant. First was the ability to cast highly complex metal works using alloyed copper and the lost wax method, which enabled Chalcolithic metalworkers to produce prestige metal objects to be used by elite members of the society to demonstrate social rank and power.[24] A second metal industry focused on the production of "utilitarian" work tools, such as axes, adzes, chisels, pins, and awls made mostly from local copper mined in southern Jordan and Israel.[25] A third and extremely rare industry was centered on the processing of gold and the casting of golden rings.[26]

Before copper ore could be utilized as metal to produce prestige or utilitarian metal objects, it required a series of processes. These include mining, transport, processing, smelting, and then casting the metal into a clay mold to produce the desired object. Experimental archaeology provides a better understanding for reconstructing these ancient processes. In 1997, shortly after the discovery of the spectacular Chalcolithic "Cave of the Warrior" in the Judean desert, I was invited by the NGS to advise them on this discovery and the nature of the Chalcolithic period in the Holy Land. During our discussions, a number of topics came up, including metallurgy, the source of Chalcolithic copper ores, mining methods, and prehistoric trade routes across the desert. I explained that all of the Chalcolithic sites bearing evidence of ore smelting and metal production had been found in Israel's Beersheva valley, and scientific analyses revealed that the copper ores used in utilitarian work tools came from Jordan's Faynan district, over 150 kilometers to the east of the site. Strangely, even today, no Chalcolithic sites have been found in the Faynan copper ore source area after many detailed archaeological surveys. Many questions arose—why there was no evidence of smelting at the source area, how ore was mined, how it was transported across the Jordanian and Israeli deserts, and how smelting was actually carried out some six thousand years ago. An editor at *National Geographic* magazine suggested that I try to answer all these questions by leading an NGS experimental archaeology expedition that focused on

FIGURE 3.11

This metal horn-shaped vessel was found with the hoard. It is similar in form to the ceramic cornet cups found at many Chalcolithic sites in the southern Levant. The horn is hollow from the mouth to the lowest line of protruding knobs, and the carefully twisted base remains a mystery.

Copper. Height 14 cm, width 13 cm, diameter 4.9 cm, weight 335 gr.
IAA 1961-169.

Photograph courtesy of Israel Museum.

these issues. When NGS offered to sponsor the expedition, I immediately contacted a number of international scholars who were eager and enthusiastic to make the journey. The international team included researchers from Jordan (Dr. Mohammad Najjar), Israel (David Alon, Dodik Shoshani, Izat Abu Rabia, and Avener Goren), Germany (Professor Andreas Hauptmann), and the United States (Thomas Levy and Pierre Bikai) on a ten-day donkey caravan to reconstruct the ancient methods of mining, transport, and smelting of ores used during the fifth millennium BCE in the Holy Land.

FIGURE 3.12A

Crown. Ten copper crowns were discovered in the treasure, all of which are similar in shape but differ in decoration. Although fairly simple, this cylindrical example has a narrow ledge rim with two schematic horned animal heads, which probably represent gazelle, each about 2.5 centimeters in height. The holes at the bottom of the crown may represent casting defects.

Copper. Height 9 cm, diameter 17.3 cm, weight 1,285 gr. IAA 1961-175.

Photograph courtesy of Israel Museum.

FIGURE 3.12B

Copper scepter. Over one hundred of these symbols of rank and power were found in the Cave of the Treasure; none are of equal size or identical decoration. This example has a disk-shaped upper rim and a ring-shaped lower rim. The piriform macelike head has spiral ridges and a cylindrical neck leading to a flat top. The main shaft has zigzag groves in the main register.

Copper. Height 32.2 cm, diameter 3.1 cm, weight 493 gr. IAA 1961-40.

Photograph courtesy of Israel Museum.

FIGURE 3.12C

Piriform-shaped mace head. Mace heads like this one are the most common artifacts found in the Cave of the Treasure hoard and have been found at a number of sites throughout Israel. Many of the mace heads in the hoard have a stone or clay core, which was surrounded by a wax layer in preparation for "hollow casting." The wax model (with clay or stone core) was then encased in a clay mold. Once the wax was removed through heating, metal was poured into the mold, resulting in a metal shell that encased the clay or stone core. These weapons would have been hafted on to a wooden handle.

Copper. height 4.8 cm, diameter 4.8 cm, weight 227 gr. IAA 1961-393.

Photograph courtesy of Israel Museum.

FIGURE 3.12D

Copper scepter with double disks. This hollow scepter has a shaft decorated with an irregular grooved weave-like design. The spherical scepter head has four small double disks. The outer disks are smaller than the inner ones, giving this scepter a celestial quality.

Copper. Height 26.1 cm, diameter 1.7 cm, weight 325 gr. IAA 1961-78.

Photograph courtesy of Israel Museum.

FIGURE 3.12E

Human-head scepter. This anthropomorphic standard is the only one of its type found in the Cave of the Treasure metal hoard. It contains many characteristics typical of Chalcolithic iconography found in the Holy Land: a large "beaklike" aquiline nose, round incised eyes lacking pupils, and a slight indication of a mouth.

Copper. Height 13.2 cm, diameter 1.9 cm, weight 268 gr. IAA 1961-84.

Photograph courtesy of Israel Museum.

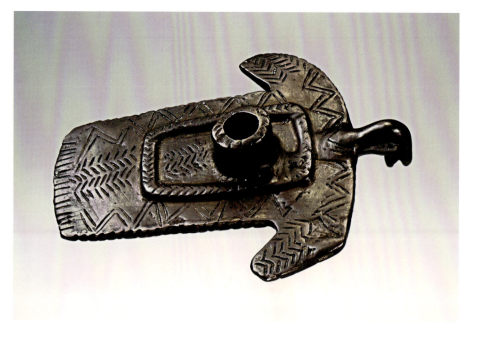

FIGURE 3.13

Vulture or eagle standard. This is a flat, rectangular-shaped, solid object. The head of the bird has holes marking the eyes and an open beak. Toward the middle of the plaque, there is a short cylindrical shaft with small projections on each side, surrounded by a raised rectangular enclosure. The herringbone designs may represent feathers. Bird motifs appear elsewhere in the hoard and on objects from other Chalcolithic sites.

Copper. Height 4.8 cm, length 15.3 cm, 597 gr. IAA 1961-151.

Photograph courtesy of Israel Museum.

FIGURE 3.14

Professor Andreas Hauptman of the GMM in Bochum is seen here using a stone implement in the Wadi Khalid to mine copper. This is a copper-rich seasonal stream bed in the Faynan region of Jordan. Hauptmann and Najjar pioneered archaeometallurgical research in this part of the southern Levant.

Photograph by Kenneth Garrett, National Geographic.

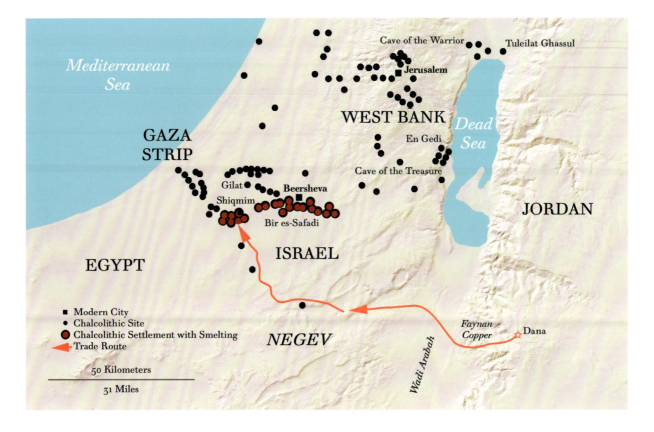

FIGURE 3.15

The ancient copper trail leading from Faynan to the Negev. The expedition of 1997, led by Thomas Levy, retraced the over 150-kilometer copper trail in the southern Levant. The expedition began in the Dana village, high up on the plateau land of Biblical Edom in southern Jordan. The team then trekked across the arid Arabah valley and through the biblical Wilderness of Zin in the Negev, to the prehistoric Chalcolithic settlement of Shiqmim in Israel.

Map by Adolfo Muniz and Thomas Levy; relief by Tibor Toth, Toth Graphix.

FIGURE 3.16

The village of Dana, in southern Jordan, is located on the edge of the Edom plateau overlooking the Dead Sea rift.

Photograph by Kenneth Garrett, National Geographic.

FIGURE 3.17

The saddlebags are laden with copper ore from the Faynan district in Jordan, the expedition team has reached the Wilderness of Zin in the Negev desert, which is midway to the Beersheva valley and Shiqmim.

Photograph by Kenneth Garrett, National Geographic.

Metal Production: Mining, Transporting, Processing, and Smelting Copper

Natural copper ore is found in three main resource areas in the southern Levant—Faynan, southern Jordan; Timna, southern Israel; and the southern Sinai Peninsula.[27] Before the ore could be processed, it had to be extracted from shallow deposits and transported to the production area. Early nineteenth- and twentieth-century explorers conducted considerable research in an attempt to identify ancient trade routes.[28] The journey described here is one of the rare recent expeditions devoted to solving these types of archaeological and historical questions (figs. 3.10–3.20).

Our journey began in late February, when a heavy ice storm hit the highland plateau of Edom, which overlooks the copper-ore-rich Faynan region. Edom is the biblical name for the region of southern Jordan that stretches southeast of the Dead Sea, past the Gulf of Aqaba (see fig. 1.3). The biblical writers most likely called the area by this name (*Edom* translates to *red* in Hebrew) because of the deep red colors of the local Nubian sandstone that make up the majority of the region's mountain geology. After inching our way for several hours over the narrow plateau roads in the four-wheel drive Chevy Suburban owned by our Israeli Bedouin driver, Izat, we reached the beautiful village of Dana, located high up on the plateau. Made of local sandstone blocks and mudbrick, Dana looks quite similar to the way in which Neolithic and Chalcolithic villages must have appeared. We reached the Royal Society for the Conservation of Nature's Dana Lodge, where we found our Jordanian partners waiting for us by the fire. In the morning ten donkeys—five for riders and five for supplies—were ready to go. Much to my surprise, the owners of

the donkeys were also determined to join us on the copper trail. By the time we set off, our team had organically grown to over fifteen individuals.

On numerous occasions I have been asked why the donkey was our transportation of choice—why not the camel, which is known as the "ship of the desert"? As this experiment was focused on reconstructing late fifth–early fourth millennium BCE mining and metallurgy, it was important to take into consideration that the camel was not domesticated in the Middle East until the second millennium BCE. The only beast of burden available during the Chalcolithic period was the donkey, which had been domesticated at the very end of the preceding Neolithic period. As pointed out by Israeli environmental scientists Michael Evenari, Leslie Shanan, and Naphtali Tadmor in their compelling book *The Negev: The Challenge of a Desert*, the humble donkey is the intimate companion of Bedouin Arabs on their wanderings, serving as private transportation, as well as leading camel caravans over the barren desert and following herds of sheep and goat over the landscape. The exceedingly modest food needs of the donkey permit it to subsist on desert thistle and straw, enabling it to penetrate the most arid deserts of the Holy Land. The donkey is also extremely well-adapted physiologically to desert life—it can tolerate dehydration of up to thirty percent of its body weight, yet its blood volume remains constant. It can also regulate its body temperature by evaporating heat at a rate that is three or four times that of the camel. In addition, the donkey's remarkable drinking capacity enables it to guzzle water at a rate of more than twenty-five percent of its body weight in several minutes. Unlike the vast arid expanses of the

FIGURE 3.18

Professors Hauptmann and Levy unpack the saddlebags containing copper ore, which the team transported from Faynan to Shiqmim. Combing the site's surface, they found an abundant collection of ancient ground stone tools, including mortars, pestles, and grinding slabs for crushing the ore.

Photograph by Kenneth Garrett, National Geographic.

FIGURE 3.19A, B

Copper production was one of the foundations of wealth finance in the Chalcolithic chiefdom of the Beersheva valley. Elites controlled valuables or prestige goods. In this case, they controlled the manufacture and distribution of copper metal objects to solidify their power within their communities and to build and maintain social networks among neighboring village elites.

Photograph by Kenneth Garrett, National Geographic.

Empty Quarter and the Arabian deserts, the deserts of the Holy Land are smaller in scale. They have natural fresh water sources, which are spread out, on average, no further than 25 kilometers from one another, thus making the modest donkey perfectly adapted to this area.

It took our donkey caravan about eight hours to descend down the Wadi Dana from the plateau to the copper ore zone that characterizes the Edom lowlands where we camped for the night. In the morning we rode into the Wadi Khalid, where years earlier Hauptmann and Najjar first discovered mines dating to the Chalcolithic period. Entering the shallow mines visible on the edge of the wadi, we used stone hammers to free the malachite ore from the massive brown sandstone host rock. After three hours of work, our saddlebags were filled with a 20-kilo sample of ore, so we rode 12 kilometers downstream to the fresh water spring at Ain Fidan, where we camped for the night.

In the morning we headed to the international border between Israel and Jordan, which runs along the middle of the very arid Arabah/Arava valley. The border is lined with antipersonnel mines, causing us to take considerable time to coordinate passage with the help of both the Jordanian and Israeli armies. Since our expedition took place only a few years after the signing of the peace treaty between Israel and Jordan, relations were new at this time. By the time we crossed, a large crowd of Israeli villagers from the settlement of Hazeva (near a spring called Ain Hosb in Arabic) greeted us and wished us well with flowers and sweets. That night we camped at Ain Tamid, around 4 kilometers west of the fortified biblical town of

FIGURE 3.22

As part of a smelting experiment, expedition party members
Avner Goren, Hauptmann, and
Levy use blow pipes made of
bamboo to keep a steady stream
of air flowing into the fire pit,
which is loaded with white-hot
charcoal. By alternating the
stream of air from one "blower"
to the next, the archaeometal-
lurgists achieved temperatures
required to smelt copper ore.

*Photograph by Kenneth Garrett,
National Geographic.*

Tamar (Hazeva). From there, it took five days to climb up the narrow wadis from
the Arava valley, across the region known in the Bible as the Wilderness of Zin,
through the Halutza sand dunes surrounding the Nahal Besor (*nahal* is Hebrew
for wadi), called the Wadi Gaza in Arabic, and finally into the Beersheva valley.
Along the way, one member of our team was thrown off his donkey and we had to
evacuate him to the hospital in Beersheva. Events like this slowed up our progress;
however, after riding for more than 150 kilometers, we reached our goal—the extensive Chalcolithic village site at Shiqmim over 10 hectares in size (approximately
24 acres) and one of the most spectacular in the southern Levant. Located in an
Israeli military firing zone, I first discovered Shiqmim in 1976 when I carried out a
survey of the Wadi Beersheva on a bicycle. For many years it was my Chalcolithic
"research nirvana," where David Alon and I excavated until 1993.

Transporting the copper ore was completed, so the next step was to process
the ore to prepare it for smelting. Following ancient methods, ore was ground into
granules using stone tools such as grinding slabs, hand stones, mortars, pestles, and
hammers. After crushing the ore, it was ready to be smelted in clay crucibles placed
on a bed of burning charcoal in a pit. Scholars debate whether furnaces were in
use at this early time. If furnaces were used, they would have been pitlike installations dug into the ground with clay-coated openings at the top. Our team made an
experimental "furnace" in this way.

Smelting refers to a process that "liberates" metal from its ore by heating the
ore beyond its melting point, which generally takes place with an oxidizing agent—

FIGURE 3.23

Pyrotechnology in action: this close-up of clay-tipped blow pipes forcing air into the fire pit illustrates how artisans increased the temperature of the fire. The introduction of air by the use of blow-pipes made of bamboo and tuyere pipes increases the temperature of the smelt. The melting point of copper is 1,083°C (1,981°F).

Photograph by Kenneth Garrett, National Geographic.

FIGURE 3.24

Quenched with water after smelting, this crucible has been removed from the fire pit. The copper metal glistens in the afternoon sun.

Photograph by Kenneth Garrett, National Geographic.

FIGURE 3.25

Andreas Hauptmann with
smelting implements used
during the experiment.

*Photograph by Kenneth Garrett,
National Geographic.*

an influx of air. In the Middle East, the first metal to be smelted was copper, followed
by iron, tin, lead, and silver.[30] During the Chalcolithic period, the process of smelting probably relied on the use of blow pipes made from hollowed-out bamboo. In
the experiments carried out on the expedition, the bamboo tips were covered in clay
to replicate the most primitive type of tuyeres and to prevent burning the bamboo
pipes (figs. 3.21–3.25). To save time in the field during the experiments, replicas of
smelting tools were prepared beforehand by Hauptmann at the German Mining
Museum (GMM) in Bochum. We carried them with us on the journey from Jordan
to Israel.

    To create an even flow of air around the crucible filled with copper ore granules,
three or four team members would alternate blowing air through our respective
pipes. It took several hours of trial and error to get the rhythm just right. Once we
did, the smelting of one crucible of ore took approximately 30 to 45 minutes, with
a net return of approximately 10 grams of copper. Since we did not have time at
Shiqmim to produce enough copper metal to cast a utilitarian tool such as an axe,
adz, chisel, or pin, we will do so in future experiments.

CHAPTER FOUR

CHIEFDOMS AND THE BIRTH OF SOCIAL INEQUALITY

Dawn of Regional Polities

After more than 1.5 to 1.8 million years of hunter-gather-forager social organization and adaptation in the Holy Land, following the Neolithic Revolution, a radically new type of social organization emerged during the Chalcolithic period, which anthropologists refer to as chiefdoms. For the first time, social inequality was institutionalized and regional systems of settlement emerged with settlement centers that coordinated social, religious, and economic activities. Based on cross-cultural studies of settlement patterns in traditional societies, anthropologist Robert Carneiro shows that chiefdoms are characterized by many special characteristics, including a two-tier settlement hierarchy.[31] Typically, large villages are surrounded by a constellation of smaller satellite villages. The larger settlement always serves as center for coordinating social, religious, and economic activities—and the residence of the chief and his family.

Based on studies of many traditional chiefdom-level societies around the world, anthropologists have determined two major ways in which chiefs manipulated their society's economy to build and consolidate power.[32] In egalitarian societies, economies are characterized by reciprocity and exchange relations between equals; in chiefdoms, it is much different. With regard to chiefly economies, one system is referred to as "staple finance," in which food surplus generated by common members is used to support a nonproducing sector of the population. These types of chiefdoms are often referred to as "Collective Chiefdoms," in which vertical relations of production and exchange dominate. The other traditional chiefly economy—wealth finance—allowed the elite to control valuables and prestige goods, which were used for exchange to solidify social relations and to demonstrate rank and power.[33] Horizontal relations dominated, and chiefs established control of labor and production. These primitive economic systems are not mutually exclusive, and there is evidence that chiefs used both systems to build their power bases.

FIGURE 4.1

Chalcolithic copper scepter with four ibex heads and possibly one goat with stylized horns. This is one of the most elaborate metal castings found in the Nahal Mishmar hoard from the Cave of the Treasure.

Length 27.5 cm, diameter 2.3 cm, weight 1,014 gr. IAA 1989-1648.

Photograph by Kenneth Garrett, National Geographic.

FIGURE 4.2 (ABOVE, LEFT)

Broken head of a cylindrical copper scepter, found as part of a foundation deposit in a large corporate building at Shiqmim. This sample has corroded to the point that there is no metal remaining in the object. Inside, one can see a thick deposit of asphalt from the Dead Sea region used to secure the scepter on a stick. The impression of the stick can be seen inside the object. The exterior of this sample has a piriform head with spiral ridges; it is identical in style to a number of the scepters found in the Cave of the Treasure hoard.

Copper. Length 8.1 cm, diameter 5 cm, weight 217 gr. IAA 1989-111.

Photograph courtesy of Israel Museum.

FIGURE 4.3 (ABOVE, RIGHT)

Split copper mace head. This mace head was found in a highly corroded state in the upper village at Shiqmim. This led researchers to saw the sample in half, only to discover that it was made of the same alloyed copper metal as similar looking mace heads found in the Cave of the Treasure. The chalk core, from a stone typical of the Dead Sea region, gives proof that prestige metal objects such as these were made locally in the Holy Land more than six thousand years ago.

Height 5 cm, diameter 4.6 cm, weight 206 gr. IAA 1989-1413.

Photograph courtesy of Israel Museum.

FIGURE 4.4

Chisel. This exquisitely crafted long narrow chisel was discovered as part of a foundation deposit in a large elite building in the Chalcolithic village at Shiqmim.

Copper. Length 20 cm, width 1.6 cm, thickness 1.2 cm, weight 178 gr. IAA 1982-1652.

FIGURE 4.5

Axe from Shiqmim. Chemical and other scientific research shows that working tools such as axes, adzes and chisels were made of pure copper ores typically found in Jordan's Faynan district.

Copper. Length 12 cm, width 4 cm, thickness 1.4 cm, weight 198 gr. IAA 1982-1654.

FIGURE 4.6

Axe from Shiqmim. Experimental archaeology carried out by the *Journey to the Copper Age* expedition team at Shiqmim showed that the large amount of time invested in producing these kinds of bifacial tools made them of great value.

Copper. Length 6.9 cm, width 2.5 cm, thickness 1 cm, 83 gr. IAA 1989-1648.

Photographs courtesy of Israel Museum.

Controlling Power through Prestige:
Copper and the Earliest Technological Monopoly

The appearance of metallurgy at this time represents not only a revolutionary development in pyrotechnology but also the emergence of social inequality in the southern Levant. The copper scepter in figure 4.1 is an example of a prestige copper metal object, more than forty centimeters in length with four crafted ibex heads and possibly a domestic goat with stylized horns attached to it. Scepters like this represent symbols of social rank and power, and new ethnoarchaeological research in India concerning the lost wax method of casting may help solve how master-pieces like this were made. A sample of three other unique copper standards from the Cave of the Treasure shows the skill and imagination of the Chalcolithic crafts people (figs. 4.2–4.6).

Wealth finance of Chalcolithic chiefdoms can be seen in the production of such prestige metal works as copper scepters, mace heads, decorative objects, and crowns. These objects were made of alloyed metal (copper, antimony, and arse-nic), which was not found locally in the Levant. Consequently, as noted earlier, the source of these objects has been highly debated by researchers. Some argue that these objects were made more than 1,000 kilometers away from the southern Levant in eastern Turkey or Azerbaijan where alloyed metal was found, and then brought or traded to Chalcolitihc sites in the Holy Land.

One mace head from the settlement center at Shiqmim, located on the banks of the Wadi Beersheva, is identical in appearance to those found in the Cave of the Treasure (see figs. 4.2, 4.3). It was made with the lost wax, or *cire perdu*, method of casting. Researchers split the sample in half to reveal a rock core surrounded by alloyed copper (see note 24). A petrographic study of the core conducted by Professor Yuval Goren of Tel Aviv University revealed glauconitic chalk—a type of rock found only in the southern region of the Dead Sea. This study, along with subsequent ones on other mace head samples with clay cores from the Cave of the Treasure, showed conclusively that local Levantine metal workers were capable of producing prestige metal work. The fact that a local rock core was covered with the alloyed metal typical of prestige metal work indicates that this object was produced locally, probably in the vicinity of the southern end of the Dead Sea. The stone core inside the mace head indicates that a hollow-casting lost wax technique was used in its production. Accordingly, the stone core was covered with about one-half centimeter of wax, the amount of metal now seen in the section of the mace head, before it was encased in a clay mold. As a result of these science-based studies of Chalcolithic metal work, it is now possible to discard the diffusion model for explaining the presence of prehistoric prestige metal work and argue for the importance of local Levantine achievements metallurgy in the production of these objects.

A second type of Chalcolithic metallurgical industry, and probably the first one to develop, was based on smelting pure copper ore to produce utilitarian tools,[34] including axes, adzes, chisels, and other tools in open molds. Numerous examples

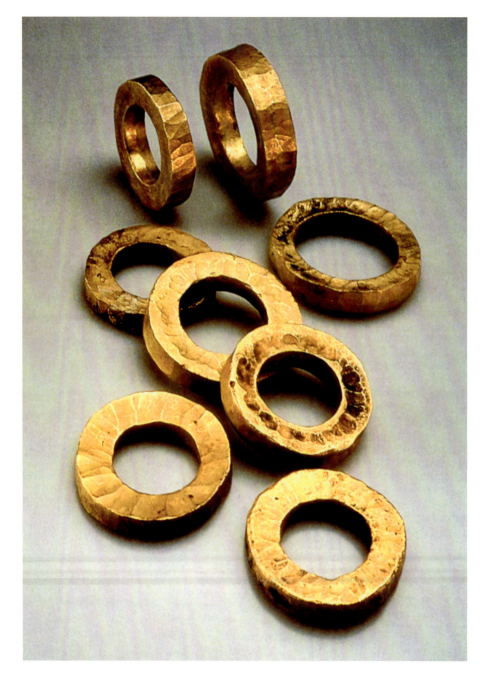

FIGURE 4.7

Earliest gold in the southern Levant. According to excavators Avi Gopher and Tsvika Tsuk, eight very similar gold and electrum rings were found in a concentration in the Nahal Qanah cave. The discovery of gold, assumed to originate somewhere in Egypt, in this Chalcolithic context highlights the long-range contact that existed amongst societies at this time. The precious metal was probably poured into open molds. When the rings were cool, a hammer was used to achieve the final appearance. For the excavators, the gold and electrum rings, in addition to the other metal and rare objects found in a burial context in Nahal Qanah, point to social ranking and possibly competition for political power characteristic of chiefdom organizations.

Average diameter approximately 5 cm, average weight 124 gr. IMJ 11237.

Photograph courtesy of Israel Museum.

of open casting molds have been found in the subsequent Early Bronze Age period at sites such as Khirbat Hamra Ifdan in the Faynan district of Jordan (see figures 7.3–7.4). These objects form part of what has often been interpreted as a household industry and are made mostly from locally available sources of copper ore found in the Faynan district and in Timna. A copper axe, such as the one in figure 4.5, weighs approximately 200 grams. Experiments carried out on the NGS Copper Trail expedition proved it would take fifteen to nineteen hours to smelt enough copper ore to produce one axe, if each smelt took approximately 45 minutes. Additional

FIGURE 4.8

A new regional Chalcolithic cultural area was discovered in the Golan Heights in the 1970s. At this site, Israeli archaeologist Claire Epstein, the discoverer of this "new" Chalcolithic culture, is shown in one of the longhouses she excavated.

Photograph by Kenneth Garrett, National Geographic.

time would be required to cast the final metal object and finish it through a series of sanding and buffing activities. The results of the expedition's smelting experiments indicate that even the production of so-called utilitarian copper objects would require labor-intensive effort. Given the fact that the ratio of copper metal axes to stone axes at Shiqmim is roughly one to two hundred and fifty, it seems that these copper bifacial tools were not just simple tools but instead were embedded with prestige and value given the labor intensive work and toil that went into producing them.

To date, all the Chalcolithic sites that have produced evidence of copper ore smelting have been found in a stretch approximately 60 kilometers (37 miles) extending along the Beersheva valley in Israel's northern Negev desert (see fig. 1.2). Metal production at Shiqmim and other sites was found mostly inside courtyards associated with the largest, elite structures at the site. This may indicate that metallurgy was practiced in secluded areas and this knowledge was not freely shared. Considering the widespread nature of Chalcolithic settlement throughout the southern Levant, this restricted distribution of production sites probably indicates that the inhabitants of the Beersheva valley region had control over metal production during the Chalcolithic period—a kind of metal monopoly. These villagers most likely organized the mining expeditions to Faynan to extract copper ore and bring it back to the Beersheva valley.

A third and much rarer type of metal industry is represented in a hoard of Chalcolithic gold rings, or ingots, discovered in the late 1980s in a limestone cave at Nahal Qanah, deep in the Judean hills (fig. 4.7). These artifacts represent the earliest cast gold objects discovered to date. Each ring measures about seven centimeters in diameter. The discovery of these objects by Professor Avi Gopher and Tsvika Tsuk of Tel Aviv University adds another type of metal technology to the list of Chalcolithic craft specialization. These researchers argue that the gold and other objects found in this burial cave strengthen the assumption that those who were buried there were individuals of high social rank in a society where status and competiton for political power played an important role.

FIGURE 4.9

Overview of the excavation
at the Shiqmim Chalcolithic
settlement center, Negev desert,
Israel. The stone wall lines less
than 30 centimeters below
the site surface represent the
foundations of prehistoric mudbrick buildings. By 1993, an
excavation area of about 4,300
square meters was exposed,
providing an excellent view
of the layout and stratigraphic
history of this settlement center.
The expedition camp can be
seen in the background.

*Photograph by Thomas Ludovise and
Thomas Levy.*

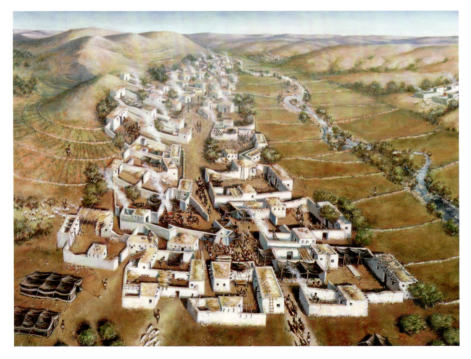

FIGURE 4.10

National Geographic artist
Chris Klein made this reconstruction of the Chalcolithic
village center at Shiqmim.
The painting is based on the
distribution of stone foundation
walls and other features. Based
on paleoenvironmental data,
the wadi environment is shown
as a narrow perennial stream
flowing through a rich alluvial
flood plain. This stream water
could have been diverted for
simple flood-water irrigation
(also called "basin irrigation").

*Painting by Christopher A. Klein,
National Georgraphic Society.*

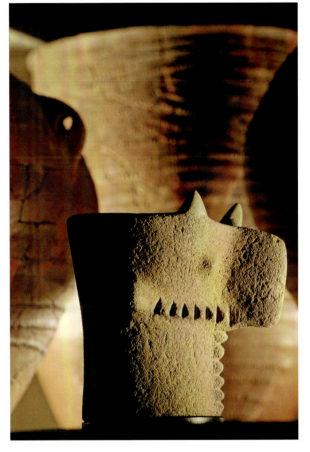

FIGURE 4.11

Anthropomorphic statuettes made of ivory were found at various Chalcolithic sites along the Wadi Beersheva. These "Pinocchio" figures measure about 30 centimeters in length and highlight the same symbolic system operated throughout this regional chiefdom organization. They also show another remarkable dimension of Chalcolithic craft specialization—the carving of ivory figures—which emerged during this formative period.

The two figures on the left were discovered at Bir es-Safadi near Beersheva; the female figure is of unknown provenance.

Photograph by Kenneth Garrett, National Geographic.

FIGURE 4.12

Cultic pillar figurine. Pillar figures with anthropomorphic features such as large aquiline noses, eyes, and ears are commonly found at Chalcolithic village sites on the Golan Heights. Most of these figures combine zoomorphic features such as horns and raised ridge patterns that may represent facial hair. The large recessed depression on the top of the head was probably used to burn offerings of some kind.

Basalt. Height 22 cm, diameter 21 cm. IAA 1987-911.

Photograph by Kenneth Garrett, National Geographic.

Chiefdoms: Regional Developments

For the first time, widespread human settlement occurred in most of the ecological zones of the region from the Golan Heights to the north with its moist Mediterranean climate to arid desert zones of the southern deserts of the Negev and Sinai (fig. 4.8). Unlike the preceding Neolithic period, which was characterized by autonomous or independent villages, societies were now organized in regional polities or cultural groups. While the causes for this striking increase in population are widely debated by researchers, the most evident change is the rise of networks of villages and farmsteads that occurred for the first time in these diverse regions.[35] One of the important questions surrounding the issue of population increase remains: How did human groups cope with this fundamental change, which caused competition over natural and social resources?

While Chalcolithic sites have been excavated in all the regions of the southern Levant, the Beersheva valley has been the most intensely investigated (figs. 4.9, 4.10). Major excavations have taken place around the city of Beersheva at Abu Matar,[36] Bir es-Safadi,[37] and Horvat Beter.[38] Approximately 16 kilometers downstream at Shiqmim, major excavations were carried out in the 1980s and 1990s by a joint team of archaeologists from UCSD and the Hebrew Union College—Jewish Institute of Religion (HUC-JIR) in Jerusalem (under my direction in association with David Alon of the Israel Antiquities Authority [IAA]).

Similarities in artifact styles of pottery, art, or ritual objects help to identify and connect human settlements to cultural areas or regional groups. Certain signature objects, such as the "Pinocchio" figures of the Beersheva valley, are often found in one specific region or cluster in one region.[39] These stylistic distribution patterns help archaeologists define the extent of ancient tribes, cultural areas, chiefdoms, and more complex social organizations. For example, the "signature" iconographic theme of the Golan Chalcolithic culture is the cultic pillar figures found in most of the longhouses that have been excavated (figs. 4.11, 4.12).[40] These anthropomorphic figures are made of basalt stone and typically have horns, very large noses (a favorite Chalcolithic motif throughout southern Levant), ears, eyes, and applied decorations, while they lack well-defined mouths (fig. 4.13). The distribution pattern of these unique sculptures indicates a unified ancient cultural area that resided on the Golan plateau.

A stone figurine head found at Shiqmim represents a portion of a Pinocchio figure that is quite similar to the ivory figures discovered at sites around the city of Beersheva in the 1950s (see note 39 [Levy and Alon]), which suggests that Shiqmim and the other sites along the Wadi Beersheva belonged to the same regional cultural system. The fact that this figurine was made from basalt, a nonlocal stone, suggests

FIGURE 4.14 (OPPOSITE)

V-shaped bowl. This type of small bowl is one of the hallmarks of Chalcolithic pottery assemblages in the north Negev, Jordan Valley, and other regions of the southern Levant. Bowls of this type, with their typical wheel marks, are the earliest evidence for the use of the potter's wheel in the region and provide some indication of mass production during this formative period. Found at Shiqmim.

Ceramic. Height 6 cm, diameter 12 cm. IAA 1980-561.

Photograph courtesy of Israel Museum.

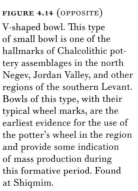

that the artist(s) went to great effort to procure a valued material for this art or ritual work.

Stylistic similarities in both ceramic and basalt vessels are another indication of cultural affiliations (fig. 4.14, 4.15).[41] The V-shaped ceramic bowl is representative of the most common Chalcolithic artifact found in the Beersheva valley (see fig. 4.14). These represent the earliest example of wheel-thrown pottery in the Holy Land and another indication of emergent craft specialization at this time. Archaeologist Yorke Rowan of the Smithsonian Institution has made wide-ranging studies of Chalcolithic basalt vessels (see fig 6.12c). The production of stone vessels is a labor-intensive task and yet another example of craft specialization.

Cream ware pottery vessels, so named because of the creamy white clay used to make them, were first studied in-depth by Israeli archaeologist Ruth Amiran, who identified them at sites extending from biblical Gezer in the Shephela hills to the northern Negev. Petrographic studies by Yuval Goren have shown that the vessels were made primarily from clays with chalk from the Eocene epoch typical of the northern Negev, which is the most likely place these fine wares were produced.[42] The distribution of unique types of ceramic vessels, such as cream ware, provides archaeologists with important clues concerning ancient patterns of trade and exchange.

FIGURE 4.15

Cream ware hole-mouth jar. These vessels are made with fine clays typical of the northern Negev region. They are relatively rare in the archaeological record of the southern Levant and were probably an important trade item from the northern Negev to other regions. Discovered at Shiqmim, northern Negev desert.

Ceramic. Height 12 cm, diameter 8.5 cm. IAA 1980-569.

Photograph courtesy of Israel Museum.

CHAPTER FIVE

FOOD FOR THE MASSES

Innovations in Storage

Based on studies of many traditional chiefdom level societies around the world, anthropologists have determined two major ways in which a chief could manipulate his society's economy to build and consolidate social power. The economy of an egalitarian society is characterized by reciprocity (sharing) and exchange relations among equals; however, the economy in chiefdoms works in a much different way. With regard to chiefly economies, anthropologists Allen Johnson and Timothy Earle refer to "staple finance," where food surplus generated by common members is used to support a nonproducing sector of the population.[43] Often referred to as "Collective Chiefdoms," vertical relations of production and exchange dominate. "Wealth finance," the other type of traditional chiefly economy, enables the elite to control valuables and prestige goods, such as those made of metals, imported feathers, rare gems, and so on. Prestige goods are used for exchange to solidify social relations and to demonstrate rank and power. Horizontal relations dominate in these "Individualizing Chiefdoms," and as a result, chiefs are responsible for establishing control of labor and production. Oxford archaeologist Chris Gosden refers to theses types of exchange as creating situations of social debt, and hence, chiefdoms can be viewed as "debt-based" societies. These two economic principles are not mutually exclusive, as seen in the Beersheva valley Chalcolithic chiefdom. There are archaeological correlates for each of these economic "types." For example, staple finance is exemplified in the archaeological record by widespread evidence of centralized control of food storage. Wealth finance is demonstrated when chiefly elites are shown to control craft specialization. Archaeologists have found evidence of both of these systems in the Beersheva valley.

Excavations and geophysical surveys have demonstrated widespread centralized storage of grain, as well as the control of copper metal production by elite groups in the Beersheva valley. In the 1950s French archaeologist Jean Perrot discovered a number of Chalcolithic villages around the city of Beersheva with networks of underground rooms and tunnels (figs. 5.1–5.3).[45] Over the years, researchers have debated what function these enigmatic "ant farm-like" troglodyte settlements served.[46] At Shiqmim, Levy and Alon led a team of UCSD and HUC-JIR archaeologists that discovered important links between underground architecture, defense needs, adaptation to the local semi-arid environment, and food storage. Assuming that the primary function was for storage of grains, the Beersheva valley case study shows that both chiefly economies (wealth- and staple-based) worked together to promote

FIGURE 5.1

A night view of some of the underground rooms excavated at Shiqmim. These subterranean structures were used primarily for storing foodstuffs such as barley and wheat. For scale, note the people sitting near the campfire above the rooms.

Photograph by Kenneth Garrett, National Geographic.

FIGURE 5.2

The photograph above shows an overview of the excavations of several subterranean room complexes in the western sector of the Shiqmim village. For safety reasons, the excavators removed the ceiling of these rooms to prevent collapse. The main function of these underground networks seems to have been the storage of grains to provision the population during times of drought. At different points in time, however, they may have been used as hidden underground defense networks and architectural adaptations to a semiarid environment.

Photograph by Thomas Levy.

FIGURE 5.3 (ABOVE, RIGHT)

In this *National Geographic* painting of an underground room complex at Shiqmim, the linkage between the above ground buildings and the subterranean rooms and tunnels can be seen. Like a "human ant farm," these subterranean systems could be used for storing foodstuffs, defense, escaping the hot desert environment, and other activities.

Painting by Christopher A. Klein, National Geographic Society.

the status of the chiefly elites in this society. As will be shown below, by using science-based research methods such as Geographic Information Systems (GIS) and geophysics, it is possible to answer many questions concerning the nature of ancient social organizations and human adaptation.

Levantine Archaeology in the Twenty-First Century: Controlling Space and Time

The archaeologist's ability to plot locations of artifacts in an archaeological site and accurately date each artifact is the key to reconstructing the social meaning of ancient material culture. UCSD archaeologists, working in collaboration with the university's California Institute of Telecommunications and Information Technology (Calit2), are helping promote rigorous methods to "control" space by employing the digital mapping capabilities of GIS in their field work in Jordan.[47] Locations of thousands of archaeological artifacts are recorded during the course of an excavation with Global Positioning System (GPS) technology using digital survey tools; they are then downloaded into a GPS program to achieve three-dimensional control of artifact location down to several millimeters accuracy. These data can then be analyzed spatially to identify significant ancient human behaviors. To achieve more dating precision, the UCSD team collaborates closely with the radiocarbon laboratories at the University of Oxford in England, the University of Groningen in the Netherlands, and the University of Arizona in Tucson.[48] High precision radiocarbon dating, coupled with Bayesian statistical analyses, enables archaeologists to measure time at the subcentury level—a critical tool that enables researchers to test the relationship between the archaeological record and ancient textual data such as the Bible and other historical documents.

Science-based methods of research currently provide important additions to the archaeologist's toolbox. By the early 1990s, it was unclear how much underground architecture was present at Shiqmim. While over twenty subterranean rooms were discovered during the course of excavation, all of them were clustered in one part of the over 24-acre site. To test the extent of these subsurface structures at Shiqmim, the late Professor Alan Witten from the Department of Geology and Geophysics of the University of Oklahoma joined the UCSD–HUC-JIR team. Witten developed

FIGURE 5.4

UCSD students helping to lay an array of "geophones" over one of the hills at Shiqmim to carry out a geophysical survey to detect underground rooms at the site. The system used—Geophysical Diffraction Tomography (GDT)—was developed by the late Professor Alan Witten. It enables researchers to translate digital geophysical data into three-dimensional images.

Photograph by Thomas Levy.

FIGURE 5.5

Using a three-dimensional computer program called "EarthVision," archaeologists were able to model underground features at Shiqmim. Here, the 5 x 5 meter excavation grid that covered the hill (known as "Area X") is shown with one 5 x 5 meter square culled out for modeling. The parallel lines show where the students establish "geophone" sensors. The blue features indicate the beginning of an underground tunnel.

Image courtesy of the family of Alan Witten, Shiqmim Project.

Geophysical Diffraction Tomography (GDT), a method for making a hologram within the earth that results in three-dimensional imaging of underground features.[49] His discovery of the world's largest dinosaur, the Seismosaurus, using GDT inspired scenes in Steven Spielberg's movie, *Jurassic Park*. At Shiqmim, GDT enabled archaeologists to test theories about the economy of a Chalcolithic chiefdom (figs. 5.4–5.6).[50] By imaging a hilltop in the Shiqmim village that was over 300 meters (almost 1,000 feet) east of the main cluster of subterranean rooms and tools, Witten discovered that the faraway hill was riddled with underground rooms. Based on the known storage function of excavated subterranean rooms at the site, the images of unexcavated underground structures can be interpreted as mostly storage facilites and an important part of the staple economy.

Innovations in Agrotechnology

The expansion of permanent settlement into the arid zones of the southern deserts of Israel was accompanied by important changes in agrotechnology.[51] Most notable is the earliest evidence of floodwater farming seen in the distribution of small Chalcolithic "check dams," which provided additional sources of water for simple irrigation farming and small gardens. Paleobotanical data from microscopic plant phytoliths adds important scientific information supporting the contention that

FIGURE 5.6

Using "EarthVision" and the data collected by Professor Witten's geophysical survey team using GDT, the entire interior of the hill in Area appears to be riddled with underground rooms and tunnels. Anthropological models and archaeological remains suggest that these subterranean rooms were used primarily to centrally store grain (mostly barley) to tide the community over in times of environmental stress. These activities reflect the use of "staple finance" by the Shiqmim chiefdom to solidify its sociopolitical power.

Image courtesy of the family of Alan Witten, Shiqmim Project.

Chalcolithic farmers used irrigation. Phytoliths are microscopic particles of minerals that form in plants and are highly resistant to decompensation. Subsequent
decay of plants releases phytoliths into soils; analysis of the phytoliths from cultural
and natural contexts yields information on both plant use by people and the natural
vegetation of an area. Arlene Rosen, archaeologist from the University College
London, studied the plant phytoliths from Shiqmim and has shown conclusively
that crops were grown under irrigated conditions as early as 4200 BCE.[52] Remarkably, in the mid-twentieth century, the necessity of providing innovative means of
farming in the desert led Israeli farmers from Kibbutz Hazerim, not far from the
Chalcolithic villages along the Wadi Beersheva, to invent "drip irrigation." Modern
drip irrigation requires the use of intricate plastic pipes and fittings to deliver water
to individual plants; this technique is widespread in the desert regions around the
world, including San Diego County and other semiarid and arid locations. It is also
possible to track aspects of ancient agricultural practices by studying assemblages
of artifacts related to the farming and processing of food. A group of artifacts from
a Chalcolithic village site in the Golan Heights shows that grain was both harvested
and processed (figs. 5.7–5.9). Other new developments in agrotechnology at this
time were the domestication of the date, the intensified use of the domestic olive,
and horticulture farming. A team led by Edwin van den Brink of the IAA recently
discovered large caches of domesticated olives at Modi'in.[53] Relying on data from

Chalcolithic sites in Jordan, the team pointed out a very important set of finds that demonstrated the widespread phenomenon of olive oil production during the Chalcolithic period. This is the discovery of large amounts of waste from olive pressing, the so-called *jift* in Arabic.[54] Daniel Zohary presented unambiguous evidence of the domestication of the olive that appeared in the Chalcolithic period.[55] More recent DNA studies confirm that olives were first domesticated in the Holy Land, with the practice gradually spreading westward across the Mediterranean basin.[56] The beginnings of fruit growing and horticulture crystallized during the Chalcolithic period, laying the foundation for an important component of the Mediterranean farming economy of today. Researchers have found evidence of Chalcolithic olive presses. One example was located near Abu Hof, a large Chalcolithic village center in the northern Negev desert. The crushed olives would settle to the bottom of the mortar closest to the man's hands. Water would have been added to float the oil to the top of the stone hole, where it would flow though the spout (connecting the two holes) and into a ceramic vessel. Organic residue analysis of ceramic vessels by Margie Burton, such as the large torpedo-shaped jars found at the Gilat Chalcolithic sanctuary, demonstrate that these vessels held olive oil. Biblical and other ancient Near Eastern texts highlight the ritual significance of olive oil in this region. Thus, the torpedo jars, filled with olive oil, were probably brought to Gilat as offerings more than six thousand years ago.

Secondary Products Revolution

New strategies for the exploitation of animals for products such as milk and wool helped transform societies when they evolved during the fifth millennium BCE. This change is embodied in the concept known as the "Secondary Products Revolution," a model coined by British archaeologist Andrew Sherratt to describe an essential shift in the way that domestic animals were exploited.[57] It is well documented that the domestication of plants and animals such as sheep, goat, cattle, pig, and equids was well established by the end of the Neolithic period (around 4500 BCE), when animals were raised primarily for meat. According to Sherratt, however, in some places in the Old World during the late fifth–early fourth millennium BCE, there was a deep-seated change in the exploitation of domestic animals (with the exception of pigs), primarily from meat consumption and hide production to the exploitation of their secondary products such as milk, wool, hair, and traction for pulling plows and early wheeled vehicles. The evidence for this fundamental change can be identified in the slaughter patterns of caprines (sheep and goat), and mostly in artistic depictions (for example, from the Sumer civilization in Mesopotamia during the

Uruk period, which shows plowing, milking, and wheeled carts). Sherratt argued that it was population growth and the movement into marginal environments that promoted the more intensive exploitation of livestock. More recent residue analyses of ceramics from Neolithic sites in the eastern Mediterranean by a team led by Professor Richard Evershed of the University of Bristol in England shows that milking may have begun as early as the sixth millennium BCE and filtered down into the southern Levant over an unknown period of time. Archaeologists working in the Holy Land have documented evidence for the Secondary Products Revolution during the Chalcolithic period.[58] These changes in animal exploitation helped promote the emergence of specialized pastoral nomadism and were accompanied by new developments in agrotechnology, such as floodwater farming and horti-culture—the widespread growing of fruits such as dates, olives, and other species noted above. It is still possible to observe many traditional Middle Eastern Bedouin societies and others who continue to exploit herd animals in ways that were estab-lished over six thousand years ago.[59]

Archaeologists rarely find artifacts that reflect major new economic trans-formations; however, as early as the 1920s, when the Chalcolithic period was first defined at the type site of Tuleilat Ghassul in Jordan,[60] enigmatic bird-shaped ves-sels were discovered, which were only later defined as milk churns (figs. 5.10–5.12). The crystallization of the Secondary Products Revolution during the Chalcolithic period brought with it more intensive exploitation of milk from herd animals, which is reflected in the numerous ceramic churns found on Chalcolithic sites throughout the southern Levant.

FIGURE 5.12

Recent residue studies of churns from Israel indicate that they were used in connection with milk. Thus Chalcolithic churns represent not only a special function but a major change in the agroeconomy of this period. This example comes from the area around the modern city of Beersheva.

Ceramic. Length 52.5 cm, height 36 cm, width 24 cm. IAA 1992-1193.

Photograph courtesy of Israel Museum.

FIGURE 5.13

Goat hair is first spun on a spindle whorl and then woven in long strips on the ground loom. It is then sewn together to make a tent over 7 meters in length. This activity is taking place in the Bedouin village of Faynan, southern Jordan.

Photograph by Thomas E. Levy.

FIGURE 5.14

A Negev Bedouin girl outside her family's tent is spinning goat hair into black yarn, which will be used to manufacture long segments of a black goat-hair tent used by the Bedouin during the winter months. Goat hair expands when it is wet; therefore, it makes a wonderful waterproof shelter for these desert nomads.

Photograph by Kenneth Garrett, National Geographic.

FIGURE 5.15

A Bedouin woman from the Negev surrounded by her children as she makes a rug for the family tent. This woman is using a ground loom to produce the rug; the ground loom is the oldest example of weaving technology and may extend back as far as the PPNB period, about 7500–6500 BCE.

Photograph by Kenneth Garrett, National Geographic.

Seeds of the Fiber Revolution

One of the most important changes in the rise of complex societies in the Middle East was the development of social groups with differential access to production-related resources. In studies concerning the rise of civilization, anthropologists have questioned why women seem to have disproportionately lost access to productive resources through time from the relatively egalitarian societies during the Neolithic period to state level societies during the Early Bronze Age in Mesopotamia (modern Iraq and southwestern Iran around 3500 BCE). In an innovative study by Joy McCorriston entitled "The Fiber Revolution," the author documents how the development of Early Bronze Age textile workshops in Mesopotamia led to the alienation of women producers in the ancient Near East and the development of Mesopotamia's political economy.[61] The transformation involved a shift from relatively self-sufficient communities into a highly integrated complex of rural and urban settlements, where textile workshops associated with temples usurped village-based subjugated and self-sufficient women workers for the aims of the temple economies. With the rise of temples in the southern Levant during the Chalcolithic period, the seeds of the Fiber Revolution began to take root at Gilat in the northern Negev desert. The presence of large quantities of tools for spinning, such as spindle whorls used for spinning goat hair and sheep wool into yarn, go well beyond the needs of single families (figs. 5.13–5.17a, b). Instead, the widespread distribution of spindle whorls around the sanctuary indicates that the production of textiles went far beyond what anthropologist Marshall Sahlins refers to as the "Domestic Mode of Production."[62] The specialization in textile production at Gilat is part of the larger Chalcolithic response to the Secondary Products Revolution, which was so fundamental to socioeconomic changes during the late fifth and fourth millennium BCE. Textile discoveries in the Cave of the Warrior in Israel's Judean desert reflect many of these changes.

The Cave of the Warrior was discovered in 1993 near Jericho in Wadi el-Makkukh (figs. 5.18–5.23a-e).[63] The site contained a unique burial assemblage that included unusual textiles, sandals, and the oldest bow preserved in the Middle East. The assemblage of textiles provides a unique window on the achievements in textile manufacture attained during the Chalcolithic period, highlighting the beginning of the Fiber Revolution, which crystallized several hundred years later in the Middle East.

FIGURE 5.16A, B (ABOVE, LEFT)
These tabular or fan-shaped scrapers are one of the "hallmark" signature artifacts of Chalcolithic and Early Bronze Age sites in the southern Levant. There are conflicting theories about their function. Some researchers suggest that they were used as butchering knives, while others argue they were used as wool shears by early pastoralists. T. E. Lawrence (also known as Lawrence of Arabia) observed Bedouin in the early twentieth century using this type of flint knives for shearing sheep. Found at Gilat

Flint: diameter 7.6 cm. IAA 1975-1122. Flint: length 9.6 cm IAA 1975-1125.
Photograph courtesy of Israel Museum.

FIGURE 5.17A, B (ABOVE, RIGHT)
A selection of finely worked stone spindle whorls from Gilat used for spinning goat's hair and sheep's wool into yarn. Different size diameter holes in ceramic as opposed to stone spindle whorls may indicate that the smaller samples were used to spin flax and the larger for goat hair and wool. At Gilat, the large number of spindle whorls found around the sanctuary suggests that spinning took place at levels well beyond the domestic mode of production. Some archaeologists suggest that the round examples were flywheels for drills.

Stone. Average diameter 5.2 cm. IAA 1975 1061, 1064-65, 1130. Ceramic. Average diameter: 4 cm IAA 1976-2, 1976-3.
Photograph courtesy of Israel Museum.

FIGURE 5.18

A detail of a "sash" textile found in a burial bundle in the Cave of the Warrior. The cloth is made of linen threads, which are spun and plied in an S direction. The piece was originally about 1.98 meters in length and approximately 20 meters in width.

Photograph by Kenneth Garrett, National Geographic.

FIGURE 5.19

Archaeologists take a break from exploring the area around the Cave of the Warrior in the Judean desert, sitting at the entrance of the cave. The discovery team was led by Dror Barshad and Idan Shaked, under the auspices of the IAA.

Photograph by Kenneth Garrett, National Geographic.

FIGURE 5.20

This skeleton of an adult male, shown here in the laboratory, was discovered with a bow and other grave goods, leading the archaeologists to dub the site as the Cave of the Warrior.

Photograph by Kenneth Garrett, National Geographic.

FIGURE 5.21

Israel Museum researcher Tamar Schick and conservator Olga Negnevitsky examine the center of one of the longest prehistoric textiles discovered in the southern Levant. This sample is over 5 meters long and is made up of multiple colored yarns.

Photograph by Kenneth Garrett, National Geographic.

FIGURE 5.22

The burial mat, bowls, large flint blade, and sandals served as grave offerings in the Cave of the Warrior. According to researchers Tamar Schick and Carmela Shimony, the objects are shown with a rectangular twill plaited mat made of split and flattened shiny reeds (*Phragmites communis*).

Photograph by Kenneth Garrett, National Geographic.

FIGURE 5.23A–E

Judean desert cave discoveries from the Chalcolithic period:

A. Carnelian beads from a necklace found in a cave in the Nahal Ze'elim region near the Dead Sea.

Faience. Average diameter 10 mm. IAA 1975-247.

B. Steatite beads from a necklace found in a cave, Nahal Ze'elim.

Stone (amber?). Average diameter 15 mm. IAA 1974-248.

C. Linen textile fragment from Cave of the Treasure.

Linen. Length 11 cm, width 15 cm.

D. Linen fragment from the Cave of the Treasure.

Linen. Length 18 cm, width 6.5 cm. IAA 1961-1271.

E. Straw mat from the copper hoard in the Cave of the Treasure, Nahal Mishmar. The mat is made of reeds (cypress). Psaach Bar Adon pointed out that "the ridges formed by the concealed weft are spaced at regular intervals, adding strength and beauty to the mat that held the metal hoard."

(Psaach Bar Adon, *The Cave of the Treasure* [Jerusalem: Israel Exploration Society, 1980], 192).

Mat fragment. Length 44 cm, width 28 cm. IAA 1961-1187.

Photographs courtesy of Israel Museum.

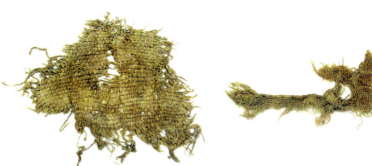

CHAPTER SIX

TERRITORIES, TEMPLES, AND CHIEFLY POWER

Cemeteries

While the earliest evidence for the symbolic burial of humans probably goes back to the Middle Paleolithic epoch (circa 250,000–47,000 BP), when Neanderthals and the first anatomically modern humans roamed the southern Levant, the earliest widespread use of special cemeteries or burial grounds that were separate from habitation sites emerged very late, during the Chalcolithic period. It is useful to consider why it took so long for human beings to conceptualize and develop a need for separate cemeteries to bury their dead.

In the Holy Land, Chalcolithic cemeteries exploded across the landscape and have been found in virtually all of the geographic zones of the southern Levant,[64] from the Mediterranean coast to the hyperarid southern Sinai Peninsula. The cemeteries are characterized by a variety of "mortuary behaviors." Along Israel's coastal littoral, caves were used or excavated into the soft sandstone ridges and secondary burial practices were common. The body of the dead was left to decompose somewhere, after which the bones of the deceased were collected and placed in fired clay ossuaries, many of which were highly decorated with paint and applied motifs. In the northern Negev desert adjacent to Shiqmim, UCSD–HUC-JIR archaeologists discovered the first Chalcolithic cemetery in the Negev.[65] Anthropological archaeologists such as Colin Renfrew have argued that the establishment of formal disposal sites or cemeteries is a clear indication of the centrality of territoriality in these formative societies.[66] Similarly, for the Chalcolithic societies of the Holy Land, the establishment of formal cemeteries is another important development connected with the emergence of social inequality and regional polities, which helped give birth of a new social "type"—the chiefdom. Cemeteries provided an important ideological expression for linking a people and its territory together.

In the Sinai desert, circular tombs similar to those found in the northern Negev have been discovered, but on a much larger, almost megalithic scale (figs. 6.1–6.3). They date to the very end of the Chalcolithic period and the beginning of the Early Bronze Age (EBI; approximately 3600 BCE). These structures are known as *nawamis* (the Arabic term for mosquitoes), and were named as such by local Bedouin. One legend attributes these structures to the tribes of Israel, who constructed them as shelters from mosquitoes. The *nawamis* of Ein Huderah (see fig. 6.1) were first systematically excavated by a team from the Hebrew University of Jerusalem, led by Professor Ofer Bar Yosef, after the Arab-Israeli War of 1967 when Israel controlled the Sinai.[67] There are forty-two *nawamis* scattered over an

FIGURE 6.1

The best-preserved *nawamis* burial field is located in the southern Sinai desert near the oasis at Ein Huderah. It was first record by the British explorer E. H. Palmer during the nineteenth century and published in his book, *Desert of the Exodus*. Following the Six Day War of 1967, Israeli archaeologists recorded seven of these burial fields.

Photograph by Kenneth Garrett, National Geographic.

FIGURE 6.2

Chalcolithic cemeteries on the coastal plain are character-ized by caves filled with clay ossuaries, or receptacles for human bones. The collection of clay ossuaries shown here were found in a burial cave at Azor, near Tel Aviv. They have anthropomorphic features and are richly painted.

Photograph by Kenneth Garrett, National Geographic.

FIGURE 6.3

This large ceramic ossuary was found in a burial cave near Ben Shemen on the coastal plain of Israel.

Ceramic. Height 40 cm, length 45 cm, width 23 cm. IMJ 82.2.558.

Photograph courtesy of Israel Museum.

FIGURE 6.4

This large loop-handled, spouted vessel with birds was found in the northern Negev desert. The birds are remarkably similar to motifs found in the Cave of the Treasure, such as the vulture standard described here. By tracing iconographic similarities between different geographic regions in the Levant, cultural connections and social relationships can be suggested.

Ceramic. Height 17.3 cm, diameter 17.8 cm. IAA 1986-339.

Photograph courtesy of Israel Museum.

FIGURE 6.5

The main cult vessels found at the sanctuary at Gilat, Israel. Shown here are the Gilat Lady, the Gilat Ram, and a beautifully painted ceramic cornet cup.

Photograph by Kenneth Garrett, National Geographic.

area of about 0.7 square kilometers at Ein Huderah. The main concentration is made up of thirty beautiful structures, separated from one another by approximately 10 to 40 meters.

Anthropological archaelogists use grave offerings as useful indices for measuring social rank and hierarchy in a cemetery. These objects also reflect the ideologies and religious beliefs of the deceased. The amount of energy (or effort) that goes into procuring raw materials and crafting objects, as well as building the mortuary structures, often reflects the status of the person who is buried in the *nawami* (figs. 6.4, 6.5). While no systematic social analysis has been done for the *nawamis* of Sinai, their uniformity in construction may indicate some kind of tribal society. The absence of evidence of permanent village settlements in the southern Sinai at this time suggests that the *nawamis* burials grounds belonged to nomadic pastoral tribes that emerged during this formative period.

Rise of the Earliest Temples

The earliest temples in the Near East emerged during the PPN period in Turkey during the tenth to ninth millennium BCE at sites such as Gobekli Tepe.[68] The question of whether Neolithic temples existed in the southern Levant is not clear, and this is a topic of intense scholarly debate.[69] Unequivocal evidence of the earliest temples in the southern Levant comes from the discovery of the first panregional ritual centers at Ein Gedi[70] and Tuleilat Ghassul near the Dead Sea,[71] and in the fields of Gilat in the northern Negev desert (see note 4; figs. 6.6, 6.7). These sites provide a rare opportunity to explore the role of religion as a critical social evolutionary force.[72] With populations growing during the late fifth millennium BCE, in addition to all the other changes in the socioeconomy of the region, the manipulation of ritual and ideology became a key factor that enabled elite members of these societies to attain social power. At Gilat and other sanctuary sites, evidence remains of

the rich interplay between the sacred and the profane. The profound socioeconomic changes that centered on the Secondary Products Revolution are reflected in ritual artifacts. Evidence of the emergence of panregional cults is shown by the production and exchange of violin-shaped figurines at Gilat, which is the site where the largest number of these exquisitely carved sculptures were found (figs. 6.8–6.11).[73] The scientific study of artifacts at Gilat has made it possible to identify prehistoric patterns of pilgrimage that were so important for integrating Chalcolithic societies at this time. By identifying the clay sources of pottery and geological sources of stone used to make artifacts such as figurines and fenestrated stands, it is possible to reconstruct these ancient trade and pilgrimage networks. Thus, the emergence of panregional temples, coupled with a variety of technological revolutions during the late fifth–early fourth millennium BCE, represent some of the hallmarks of the rise of social inequality and regional polities in the ancient Near East (see note 53). There was no turning back once this social and economic "threshold" was reached—the threshold of social inequality had been crossed; thus, the foundations of today's traditional Near Eastern society were set over six thousand years ago. The formative nature of early temples during the Chalcolithic period is highlighted by the fact that, to date, archaeologists working in the southern Levant have only discovered three of these sanctuary sites. The first sanctuary to have been discovered is located several kilometers northeast of the Dead Sea at Tuleilat Ghassul in Jordan. It was found in the 1920s by archaeologists from the Pontifical Biblical Institute in

FIGURE 6.8

Collection of violin-shaped figurines found in the Gilat sanctuary. These are made of a variety of rock types, indicating wide-ranging contacts between Gilat and other geographic regions in the southern Levant.

Photograph by Kenneth Garrett, National Geographic.

FIGURE 6.9

This large cylindrical vessel, defined as a "torpedo jar," was found with a group of similar vessels near the "Holy of Holies"—the *sanctum sanctorum* at Gilat. While over one hundred of these jars have been found at Gilat, they are extremely rare at other sites in the southern Levant. Scientific analyses of the torpedo jars help demonstrate they were used as offerings to the Gilat sanctuary. Petrographic studies show that they are made from nine different geographic regions and residue analysis indicates that they were used to store olive oil. Residue analysis of ceramic sherds from torpedo jars by Margie Burton indicates that these jars contained olive oil. These important data suggest that olive oil was brought to Gilat as offerings in these unique vessels from different olive-growing regions in Israel and Jordan.

Ceramic. Height 68 cm, diameter 10.3 cm. IAA 1987-1393.

Photograph courtesy of Israel Museum.

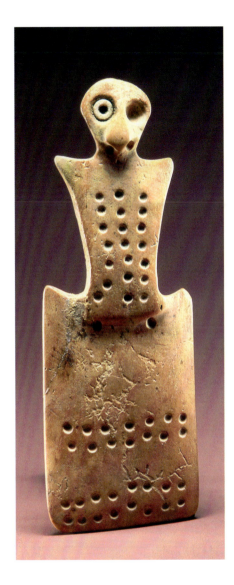

FIGURE 6.10

This human-shaped figurine made from a carved cow scapula was found in a subterranean room at Shiqmim. The figurine melds two different Chalcolithic artistic traditions—"abstract" stone, violin-shaped figurines and more representational ivory statuettes.

Bone. Height 9.5 cm, width 3.5 cm.
IAA 1996-3495.

Photograph courtesy of Israel Museum.

FIGURE 6.11

This is one of the finest examples of a Chalcolithic violin-shaped figurine. Finely sculpted from a tabular piece of sandstone, similar abstract human form figurines have been found all over the southern Levant from Lebanon to the Sinai Peninsula. The discoveries of similar figurines with breasts leave little doubt that these are representations of a female—possibly a deity. This sample was discovered near the *sanctum sanctorum* at Gilat.

Stone. Height 20.1 cm, width 7.6 cm.
IAA 1992-1212.

Photograph courtesy of Israel Museum.

FIGURE 6.12A–C (OPPOSITE)

Fenestrated stands (with windows that form legs) made of stone and pottery begins to appear in large numbers during the Chalcolithic period in the southern Levant. Based on ethnographic observations, they seem to have functioned as receptacles for hot charcoal or other materials for burning. The large basalt sample was found in the Beersheva valley. The painted ceramic stand was found with a cache of pottery vessels buried in a ritual context at Shiqmim. As basalt is a nonlocal rock type, the stone fenestrated stand was probably manufactured near the source areas in the Golan Heights, Galilee, or Transjordan, whereas the ceramic one was made locally. The fenestrated stands shown here are complemented with a well-sculpted basalt stone bowl.

A. Fenestrated stand.

Basalt. Height 23 cm, diameter 25 cm. IAA 1955-400.

B. Ceramic stand.

Ceramic. Height 22 cm, diameter 12 cm. IAA 1982-1450.

C. Bowl.

Basalt. Height 18.4 cm, diameter 40 cm. IAA 1955-401.

Photographs courtesy of Israel Museum.

FIGURE 6.13A–C
(RIGHT AND OVERLEAF)

This Gilat Lady and Ram were found together in the *sanctum sanctorum* of the sanctuary. Symbolically, these anthropomorphic and zoomorphic figures embody the new changes in prehistoric subsistence—especially the more intensive exploitation of the secondary products (milk, wool, and hair) of herd animals such as sheep and goat. The delicate cornet-shaped drinking cup was found near these statuettes and represents the kinds of vessels embedded in the back of the Gilat Ram.

A. Gilat Lady.

Ceramic. Height 31 cm, width 14.5 cm. IAA 1976-54.

Photograph courtesy of Israel Museum.

6.13B Gilat Ram.

Ceramic. Height 23 cm, length 27.5 cm.
IAA 1976-53.

Photograph courtesy of Israel Museum.

Jerusalem who were in search of the biblical sites of Sodom and Gomorrah.[74] This site has been excavated by Australian archaeologist Stephen Bourke since the 1990s. Discovered in the 1960s, the second site is near the Ein Gedi spring, which drains into the western coast of the Dead Sea and is not far from the Cave of the Treasure. Gilat, located in the northern Negev desert, is the third late fifth millennium BCE sanctuary to have been found in the southern Levant.

Of the three known Chalcolithic temple sites excavated in the southern Levant to date, Gilat has produced the richest assemblage of ritual artifacts and installations. These objects provide crucial data for identifying patterns of ritual practice, the range of ritual activities, and the contexts and conditions in which they took place. Ultimately, by understanding ritual in all these dimensions, it may be possible to understand the role of religion in social evolution.

The largest concentration of Chalcolithic sites in the Holy Land are found in the northern Negev desert, and many contain architecture and artifacts related to ritual and religion. By the fifth millennium BCE, numerous village sites expanded across the region's loessial plains; however, there was only one regional sanctuary

6.13c Cornet-shaped cup.
Ceramic. Height 24 cm, diameter 9 cm.
IAA 1987-1391.
Photograph courtesy of Israel Museum.

site—that found in Gilat. Anthropologists have shown that in traditional societies ritual permeates all aspects of life, and that it is difficult to separate the sacred from the profane. In figures 6.12a–c and 6.13a–c, some of the ritual objects found in excavations at Gilat, Shiqmim, and sites around Beersheva illustrate ritual processes such as pilgrimage, ritual practice, and regional cults that existed during this formative period.

The Metal Revolution crystallized between 4500 to 3600 BCE, with a package of new social and economic developments that ushered in chiefdoms, and with them the rise of institutionalized inequality in the Holy Land. To appreciate the long-term historical impact of these technological and social changes, it is important to have an understanding of the way in which metal production changed and became more utilitarian and mass produced in succeeding periods in the Holy Land. Helpful to this end is a glimpse at mining and metallurgy in the copper ore district of Faynan during the following Early Bronze Age—when the "Urban Revolution" took place—up until the Iron Age, or biblical period, when the first historical state-level societies emerged.

CHAPTER SEVEN

AFTER THE METAL REVOLUTION
THE EARLY BRONZE AGE

The Early Bronze Age

The impact of the metallurgical revolution that occurred in the Chalcolithic period is best understood when there is knowledge of what happened before and after it. Following the collapse of Chalcolithic societies, around 3600 BCE, there was a phase of social reorganization known as the Early Bronze Ia (EBIa; approximately 3600–3300 BCE) in the southern Levant. Populations diminished in size and settlement hierarchies disappeared. Why this collapse happened is debated; however, most likely a combination of factors contributed to this process, including a decrease in rainfall, disruption of the well-organized Chalcolithic network of mining and metal production, and perhaps military incursions by the newly emergent Egyptian state. To understand the long-term trends in social evolution and the impact of technology, ancient metallurgy can be used as a lens for examining these changes. Since 1997, UCSD and DAJ researchers have been carrying out a deep-time investigation (a study that spans vast periods of time) of ancient mining and metallurgy in the Faynan region from the time it began in the Neolithic to the first industrial-scale production in the historic biblical period of the Iron Age.

Village-Based Economies Upset the Metal Monopoly:
Wadi Fidan 4 and the Early Bronze I

Some time after the collapse of Chalcolithic societies around 3800 BCE, people living close to the ore source broke the former Beersheva valley monopoly on copper production. The site that best exemplifies the reorganization of prehistoric metal production in the Faynan region during the EBI is the site of Wadi Fidan 4, located at the gateway to Jordan's copper-ore-rich Faynan region—approximately 1 kilometer upstream from Tel Tif'dan (fig. 7.1). Wadi Fidan 4 represents the first time that local inhabitants of Faynan controlled metal production inside the Faynan copper ore district. They situated the site on an isolated, naturally defended mesa in the middle of the drainage. Excavations have revealed numerous stone lines that represent the foundations of buildings and courtyards where small-scale smelting and casting activities took place (fig. 7.2). Whereas elites sponsored metal production during the Chalcolithic period, in the subsequent EBIa, this craft seems to have been organized by individual families who resided in this small village.

FIGURE 7.1

The scale of metal production was ratcheted up exponentially by the Early Bronze II–III period in the southern Levant (about 3000–2300 BCE). Khirbat Hamra Ifdan represents the first evidence for intensive highly specialized copper metal production that went well beyond the household level and coincides with the first cities in the Levant. Thousands of casting molds, stone hammers, and other artifacts related to metal production were found here.

Photograph by Thomas Levy and Patti Rabbitt, UCSD Levantine Archaeology Laboratory.

FIGURE 7.2

Overview of the EBI (about 3600–3300 BCE) site of Wadi Fidan 4, Faynan district, Jordan. This site contained widespread evidence for small-scale household production of copper metal following the collapse of societies during the previous Chalcolithic period.

Photograph by Thomas Levy.

FIGURE 7.3

Two general types of clay casting molds were found at Khirbat Hamra Ifdan dating to the EBIII (circa 2700–2200 BCE): final product molds for axes, chisels, and pins as shown here, and molds to produce crescent-shaped ingots. These final product molds for axes are shown as they were discovered on the workshop floor dating to the third millennium BCE. These are open molds—the hot liquid metal was poured directly into the mold to form an axe. The other type are clay molds for casting small metal ingots.

Photograph courtesy of Vorderasiastisches Museum Staatliche Museen zu Berlin.

Embryonic Industrialization in the Shadow of the Earliest Cities: Khirbat Hamra Ifdan and the Early Bronze II–IV

Archaeologists working in the Holy Land have carried out deep-time studies of ancient mining and metallurgy at Timna in Israel by Beno Rothenberg and in Jordan's Faynan district. British archaeologists, led by Professor Grame Barker of Cambridge University, carried out a study of desertification and the environmental effects of ancient metallurgy on human and animal populations in the district. At the same time, archaeologists from UCSD and the DAJ spearheaded a social archaeological investigation of the role of mining and metallurgy on social evolution. By making a series of large horizontal excavations at sites such as that found at Khirbat Hamra Ifdan, it is possible for researchers to study the organization of metal craft production and its impact on social evolution (figs. 7.3-7.6). Khirbat Hamra Ifden became a major producer of copper and copper tools when the first Urban Revolution was taking hold across the southern Levant. The thousands of casting molds and other metallurgical finds enable researchers to reconstruct the *chaîne opératoire* of ancient metal production. This term, coined by French anthropologists, refers to the systematic chain of actions and processes in the production of material culture. The remarkable state of preservation at Khirbat Hamra Ifdan, probably due to an earthquake that sealed the numerous metallurgical artifacts in situ, demonstrates that this Jordanian site is the largest Early Bronze Age metal manufactory discovered to date in the Middle East.

FIGURE 7.4

The EBII–IV site of Khirbat Hamra Ifdan has produced the largest assemblage of metallurgical remains from an Early Bronze Age site in the Middle East. This display includes a selection of open casting molds for final products (pins of different size).

Height 2.5–3.2 cm, length 8–10 cm, width 3.7–6.1 cm.

Photograph courtesy of Vorderasiastisches Museum Staatliche Museen zu Berlin.

FIGURE 7.5

To store processed metal after it was smelted, the EBIII–IV metal workers at Khirbat Hamra Ifdan cast the metal into crescent-shaped ingots in brick-shaped molds. A cache of sixteen crescent-shaped ingots were found in a storeroom at the site.

Copper. Length 21.5–23.9 cm.

Photograph courtesy of Vorderasiastisches Museum Staatliche Museen zu Berlin.

FIGURE 7.6

The Khirbat Hamra Ifdan EBIII "cupcake." Ethnoarchaeological studies of traditional metal workers today highlight the importance of recycling. In the Early Bronze Age, remelting and recycling were common practice. In this cupcake-shaped conglomeration of metal, the accumulation of copper drops and small pins are evidence that small pieces of metal, as well as defective castings, were collected until there was enough metal for casting one or two ingots or other products.

6.3 x 8.8 x 8 cm. Circa 2600–2200 BCE.

Photograph courtesy of Vorderasiastisches Museum Staatliche Museen zu Berlin.

CHAPTER EIGHT

COPPER INDUSTRIALIZATION IN BIBLICAL TIMES
THE IRON AGE

Khirbat en-Nahas: An Iron Age Metallurgical Industrial Center in Jordan

By the end of the Early Bronze Age (around 2000 BCE), a time when societies were mostly nomadic pastoralists and small-scale farmers, there was a gap in metal production in Faynan throughout the Middle and Late Bronze Ages (around 2000–1300 BCE). This is ironic because the second urban revolution occurred during the Middle Bronze Age in the Holy Land, yet mining and metallurgy was not practiced in the region. During this period, the island of Cyprus had a monopoly on copper production in the eastern Mediterranean. It was not until the end of the Late Bronze Age (around 1300 BCE) that Cyprus ceased to be the main source of copper for the region. The collapse of major civilizations at this time—for example, the Hittites in Anatolia (modern Turkey), the Egyptians, and the Mycenaeans in Greece—opened new economic and social opportunities for smaller societies in the southern Levant.[75] By the beginning of the Iron Age, with the decline of Cyprus as the main source supplier of copper in the eastern Mediterranean, a boom in copper production occurred in the Faynan region. For the first time, true industrial-scale copper production was in full swing in the Holy Land. These developments coincide with biblical sources concerning David, Solomon, the Israelites, Edomites, and other peoples. Consequently, one of the hottest topics in present-day biblical archaeology is trying to understand who and how copper metal production was controlled during the Iron Age.[76]

FIGURE 8.1

In this helicopter view of the Iron Age metal factory of Khirbat en-Nahas, thousands of tons of black metallurgical slag can be seen on the site surface. The square structure in the foreground is an Iron Age fortress measuring 73 x 73 meters, which radiocarbon dates ascribe to the tenth century BCE.

Helicopter courtesy of Her Majesty Queen Noor of Jordan and the Royal Jordanian Air Force.

Photograph courtesy of UCSD Levantine Archaeology Laboratory.

FIGURE 8.2

A large administrative building (top) was discovered on the eastern margins of Khirbat en-Nahas in 2006. As shown here, four rooms were built around a central courtyard. Imported artifacts and other finds indicate that this was an administrative building linked to the Iron Age copper works. The black layers under the foundation of the building represent earlier layers of copper smelting that predate the ninth century BCE.

Photograph by Thomas Levy.

FIGURE 8.3

During the smelting of copper
ore, in addition to large con-
centrations of copper, small
"prills," such as those seen
here, accumulate as droplets
of metal inside the slag, on
crucibles and other objects.
Ultimately, prills were remelted
to form part of ingots and other
metal objects. The prills shown
here come from the Khirbat
en-Nahas.

Diameter of large prill, 3-4 mm.

*Photograph by Tim Stahl, San Diego
Museum of Man.*

The test case for understanding the organization, control, and nature of Iron
Age copper production in the Holy Land is the huge, approximately 10 hectare (24
acre) site of Khirbat en-Nahas, located in the biblical territory of Edom (present-
day southern Jordan). The site was first made famous through the explorations of
Nelson Glueck in the 1930s.[77] Andreas Hauptmann's GMM team sampled the site in
the early 1990s, and beginning in 2002, a joint expedition by UCSD and DAJ began
a series of the first large-scale excavations and surveys at the site (figs. 8.1–8.3).[78]
The new research at Khirbat en-Nahas has produced over forty high-precision
radiocarbon dates,[79] which demonstrate two major phases of copper production
at the site during the twelfth to eleventh centuries BCE, and again in the tenth to
ninth centuries BCE. No evidence of later metal production has been found at this
massive industrial site. These new data, along with the most recent excavations
carried out in 2006, are extremely important because they indicate that complex
societies, oscillating between the chiefdom and kingdom level of social integration,
were organizing the mass production of copper metal much earlier than was previously assumed by scholars. These facts create a need for new explanations concerning how and when the biblical kingdom of Edom emerged—the role played by the
neighboring kings of Israel and Judah in the production of metal at this time, and
many other anthropological and historical issues. While the new research leaves
little doubt that metal was a key factor in the evolution of Iron Age societies in
biblical Edom, many social, economic, and historical issues remain to be clarified.

CHAPTER NINE

LOOKING AHEAD

Future Directions:
Ethnoarchaeology and the Exploration of Ancient Metalworking

To understand how ancient metal production and other crafts were carried out and organized, the role of craftspeople in their societies and what the relationship between crafts and belief systems are, many anthropological archaeologists study contemporary traditional cultures around the world that continue to use technologies encountered in the archaeological record. Ethnoarchaeology—the archaeologist's study of living cultures—refers to the study of contemporary cultures with the aim of understanding the behavioral relationships that underlie the production of material culture. Using the observational methods of cultural anthropologists, archaeologists conduct ethnoarchaeological research with the aim of producing models (based on observations of contemporary societies) that are applicable to the archaeological record. I was drawn to southern India—one of the few regions in the world where traditional metal technology is still practiced—to help answer questions concerning how the lost wax method was used to produce prestige metal work found in the Cave of the Treasure and other sites in Israel, and the nature of its social function. As such, the ethnoarchaeological research that I carried out with my wife, Alina, of traditional hereditary bronze casters has important processual implications for research that concerns the deep-time study of metal production from the Chalcolithic period to the historic Iron Age. For this study, we collaborated with three brothers—Radakhrisna, Srikanda, and Swaminatha Sthapathy—who are traditional hereditary bronze casters in the Kaveri River delta region in southeast India, one of Hinduism's most sacred regions. The word *Sthapathy/Sthapati* is both a Sanskrit and Tamil term that relates to a subcaste of the Visvakarma craft clan who concentrate on the production of stone and bronze icons of Hindu gods and goddesses.

FIGURE 9.1

Ethnoarchaeology provides powerful models of analogy for interpreting the past. To study the lost wax method of traditional bronze casting, beginning in 2003, a UCSD team of archaeologists traveled to the village of Swamimalai in southern India to carry out a study of contemporary hereditary bronze casters who are expert in the use of this age-old technology for the production of religious icons. Here master craftsman Srikanda Sthapathy works on finishing a metal icon of a Hindu goddess.

Photograph by Thomas Levy.

FIGURE 9.2

Experimental archaeology in action: Master craftsman Radhakrishna Sthapathy makes a wax model of the twin-headed ibex mace head found in the Nahal Mishnar hoard in Israel. The model is based on photocopies from Psaach Bar Adon's *The Cave of the Treasure* (1980), which the ethnoarchaeology team brought to India.

Photograph by Thomas Levy.

FIGURE 9.3

Covering a wax model with clay as part of the preparation of a casting mold. A wax spout is being added to facilitate the intake of metal once the mold has been made and the wax removed. Eventually, two or more layers of clay will cover the entire wax model to make the casting mold. It is then heated to remove the wax, hence the term *lost wax* method of metal casting.

Photograph by Thomas Levy.

FIGURE 9.4

One of the best place in the
world to observe the lost wax
method of metal casting is in
the village of Swamimalai,
which is in the state of Tamil
Nadu. In this photograph
a number of workers in the S.
Devasenpathy Sthapathy and
Sons workshop prepare to move
a crucible filled with red hot
molten metal from the furnace.
Master craftsman Swaminatha
Sthapathy, in the background,
oversees the casting of two religious icons. The casting molds
are red hot and buried up to
their "gates" to facilitate pour-
ing the molten metal inside.

Photograph by Thomas Levy.

As we were interested in trying to identify the *chaîne opératoire* used in traditional lost wax metal work today to make interpretive models for Chalcolithic
metallurgy, something that had not been done previously, we traveled to southern
India. Art historians and other researchers had reported on the remarkable tradi-
tion of making Hindu religious icons in the village of Swamimalai, located in Tamil
Nadu. This is what led us to this amazing village on three different research expeditions. During 2003, 2005, and 2007, we had the unique opportunity to explore the
relationship among material culture, traditional metal technology, social organization, and exchange (figs. 9.1–9.7). This is one of the few places in the world that
preserves the lost wax method of metal production, known in Sanskrit as *madhu-
chisstavidhanam*, which was perfected around 1000 CE during the Chola Empire.
Metallurgy and the lost wax method in India go back to the Indus valley civilization,
around 2600–1900 BCE, and are not as old as that found in the Holy Land. The
artistic and technological achievements of the south Indian craftsmen that crystallized during the Chola period is unparalleled, however, and has been continued
uninterrupted by the hereditary craftsmen, known by the name Sthapathy, in the

FIGURE 9.5

Metal recyling in action.
A large ground stone mortar
is used to pulverize slag that
contains metal, prior to its
being remelted in the furnace.
Slag crushing is part of the
recycling process aimed at
obtaining any metal debris left
in crucibles or any other areas
of the workshop, which can be
remelted and used in the production of new icons. The new
UCSD research represents the
first time this important part
of hereditary bronze workshop
organization has been studied.

Photograph by Thomas Levy.

village of Swamimalai and other parts of Tamil Nadu. The Sthapathis specialize
in the production of sacred metal icons of the Hindu gods that are used in both
temple and private worship. With over one hundred and fifty bronze craftsmen in
the village, our team continues the social investigation of the workshops where
these individuals work with the aim of collecting data on the degree to which the
bronze casters are hereditary (Sthapathy), the organization of metal production,
and how metal production varies with regard to the making of metal statuary for
purposes that are sacred (Hindu temples) and profane (tourist industry). Research
from 2005 to 2007 focused on the organization of metal production. Six workshops
were visited, with one studied in detail.[80] While preliminary fieldwork provided
detailed genealogical information concerning one of the most prominent Sthapathy
families (S. Devasenpathy Sthapathy and Sons, our collaborators), extending back
some six hundred years, it is incomplete and requires more work concerning the
earliest ancestors. By 2007, our observations of the lost wax method of traditional
metal production and experimental archaeology work was completed. Toward the
end of our study season, we asked the three brothers who own the Devasenpathy
workshop, the focus of our research, if they would like to participate in an experiment
to reproduce a Chalcolithic metal masterpiece from the Cave of the Treasure. When

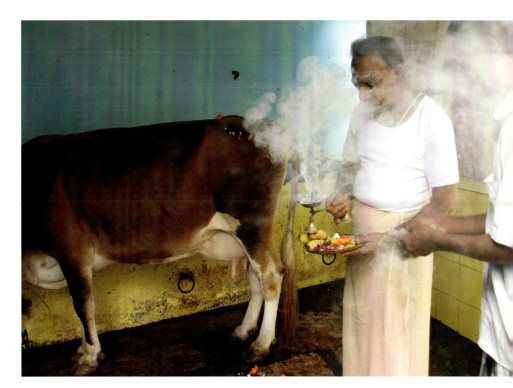

FIGURE 9.6 (OPPOSITE)

Two or more times a year, a metal recycler or "mud cleaner," is invited to large workshops to dig up the earthen casting floors and "wash" the sediment in order to extract any leftover metal bits. These are collected for recycling, placed in a crucible, and remelted in a furnace. The metal is then poured into simple molds (shallow furrows dug into the ground) to make ingots. The UCSD ethnoarchaeological study of a contemporary master craftsman metal icon manufactory in India reveals much information to archaeologists about the organization of craft specialization. This provides researchers with important models for understanding the lost wax method used during the Chalcolithic period and ancient metal working through the Bronze and Iron Ages.

Photograph by Thomas Levy.

FIGURE 9.7

Master craftsman Pranava Sthapathy conducts a *puja* ritual before casting a religious metal icon in the workshop. The cowshed is an integral part of the workshop. The sacred and the profane are deeply intertwined among the hereditary bronze casters of Swamimalai who produce sacred Hindu metal icons.

Photograph by Thomas Levy.

we only had two days left in the village, they enthusiastically agreed. By using the Swamimalai lost wax method, Radakhrisna Sthapathy was able to replicate a wax model of the famous twin-headed ibex mace head found in the Cave of the Treasure in less than two and one-half hours (fig. 9.8). Craftsmen who work in his family workshop then made a clay mold surrounding the wax model, drained the wax from the mold with heat, cast molten metal into the mold, and after cooling and breaking the clay mold open, craft the object into a final product identical to the one found in Israel dating to over six thousand years ago. Thus, our ethnoarchaeology study identified the *chaîne opératoire* of traditional metal production in south India, as well as provided an important series of models for helping to understand prehistoric metal production in the Holy Land.

There is much more ethnoarchaeological work to be done with the traditional metal workers of India and other peoples around the world who retain the art of producing many wonderful crafts, which are rapidly disappearing through industrialization and globalization. As traditional culures undergo change at an exponential rate in the wake of globalization in the twenty-first century, it is vital that anthropologists prioritize their research among traditional societies to record, analyze, disseminate, and preserve the rich tapestry of human cultures before they disappear forever.

FIGURE 9.8

The replica cast in February 2007 of the twin-headed ibex mace head found in the Cave of the Treasure. It was part of an experimental archaeology study made by the S. Devasenpathy Sthapathy and Sons hereditary family bronze casting manufactory in Swamimalai, Tamil Nadu, India.

Photograph by Tim Stahl, San Diego Museum of Man.

Conclusion

The *Journey to the Copper Age* has woven together a number of interconnected stories about the impact of technological change on the social, economic, and spiritual dimensions of humanity when the Metal Revolution began more than six thousand years ago. We have followed a group of international researchers across the deserts of Jordan and Israel to carry out experimental archaeology to more fully understand how the earliest mining and metalworking was carried out in the Holy Land. After many years of cross border archaeological fieldwork in both Israel and Jordan, we can now explain in greater detail the dynamics of how the ancient mining and metal production impacted societies, from the earliest farmers and herders of the Neolithic period, to the emergence of the first chiefdom level societies, up to the rise of the first historic kingdoms and states during the Iron Age and biblical times. For the Chalcolithic period, we have seen how a "package" of new technological, subsistence, ritual, and other developments crystallized in the emergence of social inequality. Why did it take archaeologists so long to recognize this fundamental social change? As the distinguished anthropological archaeologist Kent Flannery has shown, the reason it is so difficult to recognize chiefdoms in the prehistoric Near East is because early Near Eastern chiefdoms were not "flamboyant" like the New World chiefdoms of Mesoamerica.[81] By this, Flannery means that early Near Eastern chiefs showed little interest in elaborate dress and demonstrating their wealth through elaborate burials—the kind of material "fingerprint" that enables archaeologist to easily identify rank and power in an ancient society. Consequently, in *Journey to the Copper Age*, we have relied on a wide range of data—most importantly the Metal Revolution, to trace the emergence and organization of these early hierarchical societies in the Holy Land. Whereas a Maya chief might have relied exclusively on controlling wealth to consolidate his power, those in the southern

Levant relied on a combination of staple and wealth finance to build and maintain their coalitions. Finally, we have seen the centrality of using one of archaeology's least developed subfields of research—ethnoarchaeology—for studying contemporary traditional peoples to understand the past and preserve rich cultural heritage.

While these studies are extremely important, from an ethical point of view, archaeologists and other researchers need to consider returning something to the communities and countries in which they work. The Holy Land, including Israel, Jordan, and the Palestinian territories, contains precious cultural resources, which we, as archaeologists, are privileged to explore and research. As our research efforts have focused on the archaeology of ancient mining and metallurgy in Israel's northern Negev desert and Jordan's copper-ore-rich Faynan district, it is hoped that the interest generated by this book and the SDMM exhibition will help promote tourism, geotourism, and cultural preservation in these spectacular deserts. Of immediate concern are the dangers caused by rapid economic development in the Faynan district, which contains the best-preserved landscape of ancient mining and metallurgy in the world. Other historic regions rich with ancient metal resources have not been so fortunate, including Rio Tinto in Spain, the Troodos mountains in Cyprus, Timna in Israel, and others, which have been ravaged by modern mining. Fortunately, the Faynan landscape has not suffered greatly at the hands of major mining activities or other destruction. With the increase in the price of copper, however, the Faynan cultural resource is in danger. The best way to preserve Faynan is to have the entire 625-kilometer (km^2) area declared a United Nations Educational, Scientific, and Cultural Organization (UNESCO) World Heritage Site.

Conserving Faynan as a UNESCO World Heritage Site

UNESCO seeks to identify and preserve the world's cultural and natural heritage that is considered to be of outstanding value to humanity. The copper-ore-rich Faynan district, with its spectacular geology, landscape, and rich archaeological heritage, is one of these unique and irreplaceable cultural and natural resources. Its listing as a UNESCO World Heritage Site would stop the threat from modern mining companies and provide tourism, which would help sustain the now-depressed local economy in this part of Jordan.

Epilogue: Anthropology into the Twenty-First Century

As shown by the ethnoarchaeological research of the hereditary bronze casters of southern India discussed here, societies like these provide critical windows on the technologies, belief systems, economies, trade systems, and other dimensions of traditional cultures. Traditional societies throughout the planet represent the basic fiber that makes up the rich tapestry of our world's cultural heritage—past, present, and future. In *Journey to the Copper Age*, researchers have relied on the study of traditional lost wax metal casting technology and society in India to provide profound insights into the same anthropological issues in formative late fifth–early

FIGURE 9.9

Faynan, Jordan. The morning
mist rises over the lowlands of
Edom. The mountains of the
highland plateau can be seen
in silhouette rising up over the
desert. As the best preserved
ancient mining and metallurgy
landscape in the world, it is
imperative to protect Faynan's
rich natural and cultural
resources by making it a
UNESCO World Heritage Site.

Photograph by Thomas Levy.

fourth millennium BCE societies in the southern Levant. As researchers it is our responsibility to study, analyze, and publish our results not only for the scholarly community but to make that data available to the people we study and the "global village" in which we live. In this sense, anthropological research in the twenty-first century is not only an academic pursuit aimed at understanding human diversity but it also has responsibilities to curate both the past and present aspects of the world's cultural heritage that are in danger of disappearing. To adequately do this today, in the face of rapid technological change and globalization, we need to reach out and connect to the world community. This can be done by taking advantage of the new advances in telecommunications and information technology that have a positive "flattening" effect on the world. This Information Technology (IT) revolution enables global collaboration, understanding, and outreach on a scale that has never been seen before in history. The effect of the IT revolution on society today is as profound as the Metal Revolution was on ancient communities more than six thousand years ago. Accordingly, the video that accompanies the *Journey to the Copper Age*, which is an anthropological archaeology study of past and present metal production in traditional societies, will be archived and hosted online with the UCSD Calit2 (http://www.calit2.net). It is our hope that this will be the beginning of an online digital archive of video films concerning the world's traditional technologies that will have open access to all.

NOTES TO THE TEXT

1. Manuel Castells, *The Rise of the Network Society* (Malden, Mass.: Blackwell Publishers, 2000).
2. V. Gordon Childe, *Man Makes Himself* (London: Watts, 1936).
3. Thomas E. Levy, "Grand Narratives, Technological Revolutions, and the Past: Deep-Time Studies of Metallurgy and Social Evolution in the Eastern Mediterranean," in *Connectivity in Antiquity: Globalization as a Long-Term Historical Process*, ed. Oystein LaBianca and Sandra Arnold Scham (London: Equinox, 2006), 10–25.
4. Thomas E. Levy, ed., *Archaeology, Anthropology, and Cult: The Sanctuary at Gilat, Israel* (London: Equinox, 2006); and Thomas E. Levy, ed., *Shiqmim I: Studies Concerning Chalcolithic Societies in the Northern Negev Desert, Israel (1982–1984)*, British Archaeological Reports International Series 356 (Oxford: Archaeopress, 1987).
5. Mircea Eliade, *The Forge and the Crucible: The Origins and Structures of Alchemy* (Chicago: University of Chicago Press, 1978).
6. Colin Renfrew and Paul Bahn, *Archaeology: Theories, Methods, and Practice*, 4th ed. (London: Thames, 2004), 342.
7. Stephen J. Gould and Niles Eldredge, "Punctuated Equilibria: The Tempo and Mode Reconsidered," *Paleobiology* 3, no. 2 (1977): 115–51.
8. Kathleen M. Kenyon, *Digging Up Jericho* (London: Benn, 1957).
9. Gary Rollefson, "Neolithic 'Ain Ghazal (Jordan): Ritual and Ceremony II," *Paleorient* 12, no. 1 (1986): 45–52.
10. Hans Georg K. Gebel and H. D. Bienert, "Ba'ja Hidden in the Petra Mountains: Preliminary Results of the 1997 Investigations," *The Prehistory of Jordan II: Perspectives from 1997*, ed. Hans Georg K. Gebel, Zeiden Kafafi, and Gary Rollefson, Studies in Early Near Eastern Production, Subsistence and Environment 4 (Berlin: ex oriente, 1997), 221–62.
11. Alan H. Simmons and Mohammad Najjar, "Ghwair I: A Small, Complex Neolithic Community in Southern Jordan," *Journal of Field Archaeology* 31 (2006): 77–95.
12. Thomas E. Levy, Russell B. Adams, and Mohammad Najjar, "Early Metallurgy and Social Evolution: Jabal Hamrat Fidan," *ACOR Newsletter* 11 (1999): 1–3.
13. Ian Kuijt, ed., *Life in Neolithic Farming Communities: Social Organization, Identity, and Differentiation* (New York: Kluwer Academic/Plenum Publishers, 2000).
14. Ofer Bar-Yosef and Anna Belfer-Cohen, "The PPNB Interaction Sphere," in *People and Cultures in Change*, ed. Israel Hershkovitz, British Archaeological Reports International Series 508 (Oxford: Archaeopress, 1989), 59–72.
15. Thomas Levy and Sariel Shalev, "Prehistoric Metalworking in the Southern Levant: Archaeometallurgical and Social Perspectives," *World Archaeology* 20, no. 3 (1989): 352–72.
16. David Neev and K. O. Emery, "The Dead Sea," *Bulletin Geological Survey of Israel* 41 (1967): 1–147.
17. Glenn A. Goodfriend, "Mid-Holocene Rainfall in the Negev Desert from 13C Land Snail Shell Organic Matter," *Nature* 333 (1988): 757–60.
18. Uri Baruch, "Palynological Evidence of Human Impact on the Vegetation as Recorded in Late Holocene Lake Sediments in Israel," in *Man's Role in the Shaping of the Eastern Mediterranean Landscape*, ed. G. Entjes-Nieborg and W. van Zeist (Rotterdam: Balkema, 1990), 283–94.
19. Paul Goldberg and A. M. Rosen, in Levy 1987 (see note 4), 23–32.
20. Yuval Goren, "The Location of Specialized Copper Production by the Lost Wax Technique in the Chalcolithic Southern Levant" *Geoarchaeology* (forthcoming); Miriam Tadmor et al., "The Nahal Mishmar Hoard from the Judean Desert: Technology, Composition and Provenance," *Atiqot* 27 (1995): 95–148; and Sariel Shalev and J. Peter Northover, "Metallurgy of the Nahal Mishmar Hoard Reconsidered," *Archaeometry* 35 (1993): 35–47.
21. Catherine Commenge-Pellerin, *Poterie d'Abou Matar et de l'Ouadi Zoumeili (Beersheva) au IVe millenaire avant l'ere chretienne* (Paris: Association Paleorient, 1987); Catherine Commenge-Pellerin, *La Potterie de Safadi (Beersheva) au IVe millenaire avant l'ere chretienne* (Paris: Association Paleorient, 1990); and Valentine Roux and M. A. Courty, "Identification of Wheel-Fashioning Methods: Technological Analysis of 4th-3rd Millennium BC Oriental Ceramics," *Journal of Archaeological Science* 25 (1998): 747–63.
22. Yorke M. Rowan, "Ancient Distribution and Deposition of Prestige Objects: Basalt Vessels during the Late Prehistory of the Southern Levant," (Ph.D. diss., University of Texas at Austin, 1998); and Yorke M. Rowan, "Gilat's Ground Stone Assemblage: Stone Fenestrated Stands, Bowls, Palettes and Related Objects," in Levy 2006 (see note 4), 507–74.
23. Daniella E. Bar-Yosef Mayer et al., "Steatite Beads at Peqi'in: Long-Distance Trade and Pyrotechnology during the Chalcolithic of the Southern Levant," *Journal of Archaeological Science* 31 (2004): 493–502.
24. Sariel Shalev et al., "A Chalcolithic Mace Head from the Negev: Technological Aspects and Cultural Implications," *Archaeometry* 34 (1992): 63–71.
25. Sariel Shalev and J. Peter Northover, "Chalcolithic Metal and Metalworking from Shiqmim," in Levy 1987 (see note 4).
26. Sariel Shalev, "The Earliest Gold Artifacts in the Southern Levant: Reconstruction of the Manufacturing Process," in *Outils et Ateliers a'orfevres des temps anciens*, ed. C. Eluere (Saint-Germain-en-Laye: Societe des Amis du Musee des Antiquites Nationales, 1993), 9–12.
27. Andreas Hauptmann, "Developments in Copper Metallurgy during the Fourth and Third Millennia BC at Feinan, Jordan," in *Mining and Metal Production Through the Ages*, ed. Paul Craddock and Janet Lang (London: The British Museum Press, 2003), 90–100; Andreas Hauptmann, H. G. Bachmann, and Robert Maddin, "Chalcolithic Copper Smelting: New Evidence from Excavations at Wadi Fidan 4," in *Archaeometry '94*, ed. S. Demirci, A. M. Özer, and G. D. Summers (Ankara: Tübitak, 1996), 3–10; Andreas Hauptmann and Gerd Weisgerber, "Periods of Ore Exploitation and Metal Production in the Area of Feinan, Wadi 'Arabah, Jordan," in *Studies in the History and Archaeology of Jordan, IV*, ed. M. Zaghloul, K. 'Amr, and F. Zayadine (Amman: Department of Antiquities of Jordan, 1992), 61–66; and Andreas Hauptmann, "The Earliest Periods of Copper Metallurgy in Feinan, Jordan," in *Old World Archaeometallurgy*, ed. Andreas

Hauptmann, E. Pernicka, and G. A. Wagner (Bochum: Selbstver-leg des Deutschen Berghau Museums, 1989), 119-35.

28. Edward Robinson, *Biblical Researches in Palestine and Adjacent Regions* (London: J. Murray, 1867; reprint, Jerusalem: Universitas, 1970); and Alois Musil, *Arabia Petraea* (Vienna: Holder, 1907-9).

29. Michael Evenari, Leslie Shanan, and Naphtali Tadmor, *The Negev: The Challenge of a Desert*, 2nd ed. (Cambridge, Mass.: Harvard University Press, 1982).

30. R. F. Tylecote, *The Early History of Metallurgy in Europe* (London: Longman, 1987).

31. Robert L. Carneiro, "The Chiefdom: Precursor of the State," in *The Transition to Statehood in the New World*, ed. Grant D. Jones and Robert R. Kautz (Cambridge, Mass.: University Press, 1981), 37-79.

32. Allen W. Johnson and Timothy K. Earle, *The Evolution of Human Societies: From Foraging Group to Agrarian State* (Stanford: Stanford University Press, 1987).

33. Kent V. Flannery and Joyce Marcus, eds., *The Cloud People: Divergent Evolution of the Zapotec and Mixtec Civilizations* (New York: Academic Press, 1983).

34. Sariel Shalev, "Two Different Copper Industries in the Chalcolithic Culture of Israel," in *Decouverte du Metal*, ed. Jean-Pierre Mohen and Christiane Eluère (Paris: Picard, 1991), 413-24.

35. Thomas E. Levy, Margie M. Burton, and Yorke M. Rowan, "Chalcolithic Hamlet Excavations near Shiqmim, Negev Desert, Israel," *Journal of Field Archaeology* 31 (2006): 41-60.

36. Bar-Yosef Mayer et al. (see note 23); Jean Perrot, "The Excavations at Tell Abu Matar, Near Beersheba," *Israel Exploration Journal* 5 (1955): 17-41, 73-84, 167-89; and Aaron Shugar, "Recent Research in Chalcolithic Metallurgy: Investigation of Abu Matar, Israel," *International Mining and Minerals* 1 (1998): 114-16.

37. Catherine Commenge-Pellerin 1990 (see note 21); and Jean-Paul Perrot, "Structures D'Habitat Mode de vie et Environnement: Les Villages Souterrains des Pasteurs de Beersheva, dans le sud D''Israel, au IVe Millenaire Avant L'ere Chretienne," *Paleorient* 10 (1984): 75-96.

38. M. Dothan, "Excavations at Horvat Beter (Beersheba)," *Atiqot* II (1959): 1-42; and Steven A. Rosen and I. Eldar, "Horvat Beter Revisited: The 1982 Salvage Excavations," *Atiqot* 22 (1993): 13-27.

39. Thomas E. Levy and David Alon, "An Anthropomorphic Statuette Head from the Shiqmim Chalcolithic Site," *Atiqot* 17 (1985): 187-89; Thomas E. Levy and David Alon, "A Corpus of Ivories from Shiqmim," *Eretz Israel* 23 (1992): 65-71; and Jean Perrot, "Statuettes en Ivoire et Autre Objets en Ivoire et en os Provenant des Gisements Prehistoriques de la Region de Beersheba," *Syria* 36 (1959): 8-19.

40. Claire Epstein, *The Chalcolithic Culture of the Golan* (Jerusalem: Israel Antiquities Authority, 1998).

41. Yorke M. Rowan et al., "Gilat's Ground Stone Assemblage: Stone Fenestrated Stands, Bowls, Palettes, and Related Artifacts," in Levy 2006 (see note 4), 575-684.

42. Ruth Amiran, "The 'Cream Ware' of Gezer and the Beersheba Late Chalcolithic," *Israel Exploration Journal* 5 (1955): 244-45; and Isaac Gilead and Yuval Goren, "Petrographic Analyses of 4th Millenium B.C. Pottery and Stone Vessels from the Northern Negev, Israel," *Bulletin of the American Schools of Oriental Research* 275 (1989): 5-14.

43. Alan W. Johnson and Timothy K. Earle, *The Evolution of Human Societies: From Foraging Group to Agrarian State* (Stanford: Stanford University Press, 1987); Timothy Earle, "The Evolution of Chiefdoms," *Current Anthropology* 30 (1989): 84-88; Timothy Earle, *How Chiefs Come to Power: The Political Economy in Prehistory* (Stanford: Stanford University Press, 1997); and Timothy Earle, ed., *Chiefdoms: Power, Economy, and Ideology* (Cambridge, Mass., and New York: School of American Research and Cambridge University Press, 1991).

44. Chris Gosden, "Debt, Production, and Prehistory," *Journal of Anthropological Archaeology* 8 (1989): 355-87.

45. Perrot 1955 (see note 36); and Perrot 1984 (see note 37).

46. Isaac Gilead, "A New Look at Chalcolithic Beer-Sheba," *Biblical Archaeologist* 50 (1987): 110-17; and Thomas E. Levy, "Transhumance, Subsistence, and Social Evolution in the Northern Negev Desert," in *Pastoralsim in the Levant: Archaeological Material in Anthropological Perspective*, ed. Anatoly Khaznov and O. B. Yosef (Madison, Wisc.: Prehistory Press, 1992), 65-82.

47. Thomas E. Levy et al., "Digital Archaeology 2001: GIS-Based Excavation Recording in Jordan," *The SAA Archaeological Record* 1 (2001): 23-29; and Thomas E. Levy and Neil G. Smith, "On-Site Digital Archaeology: GIS-Based Excavation Recording in Southern Jordan," in *Crossing Jordan: North American Contributions to the Archaeology of Jordan*, ed. Thomas E. Levy et al. (London: Equinox, 2007), 47-58.

48. Thomas E. Levy and Thomas Higham, eds., *The Bible and Radiocarbon Dating: Archaeology, Text, and Science* (London: Equinox, 2005).

49. Alan Joel Witten, *Equinox Handbook of Geophysics and Archaeology* (London: Equinox, 2006).

50. Alan Joel Witten et al., "Geophysical Diffraction Tomography: New Views on the Shiqmim Prehistoric Subterranean Village Site (Israel)," *Geoarchaeology* 10 (1995): 97-118.

51. Thomas E. Levy, "The Emergence of Specialized Pastoralism in the Southern Levant," *World Archaeology* 15 (1983): 15-36; Caroline Grigson, "Plough and Pasture in the Early Economy of the Southern Levant," in *The Archaeology of Society in the Holy Land*, ed. Thomas E. Levy (London: Leicester University Press, 1998), 245-68; and Caroline Grigson, "Farming? Feasting? Herding? Large Mammals from the Chalcolithic of Gilat," in Levy 2006 (see note 4), 215-319.

52. Arlene Rosen, "Phytolith Studies at Shiqmim," in Levy 1987 (see note 4); and Arlene M. Rosen, "Preliminary Identification of Silica Skeletons from Near Eastern Archaeological Sites," in *Phytolith Systematics*, ed. George Rapp, Jr. and S. C. Mulholland (New York: Plenum Press, 1992), 129-47.

53. Simcha Lev-Yadun, Moshe Inbar, and Edwin C. M. van den Brink, "Two Six-Thousand-Year-Old Chalcolithic Olive Seed Hoards from Modi'in, Israel" (forthcoming).

54. Reinder Neef, "Introduction, Development, and Environmental Implications of Olive Culture: The Evidence from Jordan," in *Man's Role in the Shaping of the Eastern Mediterranean*

Landscape, ed. S. Bottema, G. Entjes-Nieborg, and W. van Zeist (Rotterdam: A. A. Balkema, 1990), 295–306.

55. Daniel Zohary, "Beginnings of Fruit Growing in the Old World," *Science* 187 (1975): 319–27.

56. V. Bronzini de Caraffa et al. "Mitochondrial DNA Variation and RAPD Mark Oleasters, Olive, and Feral Olive from Western and Eastern Mediterranean," *Theoretical Applied Genetics* 104 (2002): 1209–16; and M. Burton and Thomas E. Levy, "Organic Residue Analysis of Selected Vessels from Gilat: Gilat Torpedo Jars," in Levy 2006 (see note 4).

57. Andrew G. Sherratt, "Plough and Pastoralism: Aspects of the Secondary Products Revolution," in *Patterns of the Past: Studies in Honour of David Clarke*, ed. I. Hodder, G. Isaac, and N. Hammond (Cambridge, Mass.: Cambridge University Press, 1981), 261–305.

58. Levy 1983 (see note 51); Thomas E. Levy, "Production, Space and Social Change in Prehistoric Palestine," in *Spatial Boundaries and Social Dynamics*, ed. Augustin Holl and Thomas E. Levy (Ann Arbor: Monograph Series of the Journal of Anthropological Archaeology, 1993), 63–81.

59. Aref Abu Rabia, *The Negev Bedouin and Livestock Rearing: Social, Economic and Political Aspects* (Oxford: Berg, 1994); and Carol Palmer, "Milk and Cereals: Identifying Food and Food Identity among Fallahin and Bedouin in Jordan," *Levant* 34 (2002): 173–95.

60. Stephen Bourke, "The Chalcolithic Period," in *The Archaeology of Jordan*, ed. B. MacDonald, Russell B. Adams, and Piotr Bienkowski (Sheffield: Sheffield Academic Press, 2001).

61. Joy McCorriston, "The Fiber Revolution: Textile Extensification, Alienation, and Social Stratification in Ancient Mesopotamia," *Current Anthropology* 38 (1997): 517–48.

62. Marshall Sahlins, *Stone Age Economics* (London: Tavistock Publications, 1974).

63. T. Schick, ed., *The Cave of the Warrior: A Fourth Millennium Burial in the Judean Desert* (Jerusalem: Israel Antiquities Authority, 1998).

64. Edwin C. M. van den Brink, "An Index to Chalcolithic Mortuary Caves in Israel," *Israel Exploration Journal* 48 (1998): 165–73; and Jean Perrot and Daniel Ladiray, *Tombes A Ossuaires de la Region Cotiere Palestinienne, Au IVe Millenaire Avant L'eve Chretienne* (Paris: Association Paleorient, 1980).

65. Thomas E. Levy and David Alon, "The Chalcolithic Mortuary Site near Mezad Aluf, Northern Negev Desert: A Preliminary Study," *Bulletin of the American Schools of Oriental Research* 248 (1982): 37–59.

66. Colin Renfrew, ed., *The Explanation of Culture Change: Models in Prehistory* (London: Duckworth, 1973).

67. Ofer Bar Yosef et al., "The Nawamis Near Ein Huderah (Eastern Sinai)," *Israel Exploration Journal* 27 (1977): 65–88; Ofer Bar-Yosef et al., "Nawamis and Habitation Sites near Gebel Gunna, Southern Sinai," *Israel Exploration Journal* 36 (1986): 121–67.

68. K. Schmidt, "Frühneolithische Zeichen vom Göbekli Tepe: Ilk Neolitik Göbekli Tepe Betimlemeleri," *TÜBA-AR: Türkiye Bilimler Akademisi Arkeoloji Dergisi* 7 (2004): 93–105.

69. Gary O. Rollefson, "Early Neolithic Ritual Centers in the Southern Levant," *Neo-Lithics* (2005): 3–13; and Thomas E. Levy, "Comment: The View from the End of the Trajectory," *Neo-Lithics* (2005): 37–39.

70. David Ussishkin, "The Ghassulian Shrine at En Gedi," *Tel Aviv* 7 (1980): 1–44.

71. Peta L. Seaton, "Chalcolithic Cult and Risk Management at Teleilat Ghassul: Toward an Archaeology of Politics" (Ph.D. diss., Department of Classical Archaeology, University of Sydney, 2006); Peta Seaton, "Aspects of New Research at the Chalcolithic Sanctuary Precinct at Teleilat Ghassul," in *Proceedings of the First International Congress on the Archaeology of the Ancient Near East, Rome, May 18th–23rd, 1998*, ed. P. Matthiae et al., (Rome, 2000): 1503–14.

72. David Alon and Thomas E. Levy, "The Archaeology of Cult and Chalcolithic Sanctuary at Gilat," *Journal of Mediterranean Archeology* 2 (1989): 163–221.

73. Catherine Commenge et al., in Levy 2006 (see note 4), 739–830.

74. Thomas Levy, "The Chalcolithic Period," *Biblical Archaeologist* 49 (1986): 83–106.

75. J. D. Muhly, R. Maddin, and V. Karageorghis, eds., *Early Metallurgy in Cyprus, 4000–500 B.C.* (Nicosia: Pierides Foundation, 1982).

76. Israel Finkelstein, "Khirbet en-Nahas, Edom, and Biblical History," *Tel Aviv* 32 (2005): 119–25; and Thomas E. Levy and Mohammad Najjar, "Some Thoughts on Khirbat en-Nahas, Edom, Biblical History, and Anthropology: A Response to Israel Finkelstein," *Tel Aviv* 33 (2006): 107–22.

77. Nelson Glueck, *The Other Side of the Jordan* (New Haven: American Schools of Oriental Research, 1940).

78. Thomas E. Levy et al., "Reassessing the Chronology of Biblical Edom: New Excavations and 14C Dates from Khirbat en-Nahas (Jordan)," *Antiquity* 78 (2004): 863–76; Thomas E. Levy and Mohammad Najjar, "Edom and Copper: The Emergence of Ancient Israel's Rival," *Biblical Archaeology Review* 32 (2006): 24–35, 70; Thomas E. Levy et al., "Lowland Edom and the High and Low Chronologies: Edomite State Formation, the Bible and Recent Archaeological Research in Southern Jordan," in *The Bible and Radiocarbon Dating: Archaeology, Text, and Science*, ed. Thomas E. Levy and Thomas Higham (London: Equinox Publishing, 2005), 129–63; and V. Fritz, "Ergebnisse einer Sondage in Hirbet en-Nahas, Wadi el-'Araba (Jordanien)" *Zeitschrift des Deutschen Pälestina Vereins* 112 (1996): 1–9.

79. Thomas Higham et al., "Radiocarbon Dating of the Khirbat en-Nahas site (Jordan) and Bayesian Modeling of the Results," Levy and Higham 2005 (see note 78), 164–78.

80. Thomas E. Levy et al., "From Holy Land to Holy Land— Ethnoarchaeological Perspectives on Hereditary Bronze Casters in Swamimalai, South India" (forthcoming).

81. Kent V. Flannery, "Chiefdoms in the Early Near East: Why It's So Hard to Identify Them," in *The Iranian World: Essays on Iranian Art and Archaeology*, ed. A. Alizadeh, Y. Majidzadeh, and S. M. Shahmirzadi (Tehran: Iran University Press, 1999), 44–58.

INDEX

Thomas E. Levy is professor of Anthropology and Judaic Studies at the University of California, San Diego. He is the inaugural holder of the Norma Kershaw Endowed Chair in the Archaeology of Ancient Israel and Neighboring Lands. Levy has carried out major excavation projects in Israel at Chalcolithic and Early Bronze Age sites. Since 1997, his research has focused on the role of mining and metallurgy in the evolution of societies in the Faynan district of southern Jordan. Widely published, his most recent work is an edited book entitled *Archaeology, Anthropology, and Cult: The Sanctuary at Gilat, Israel.*

Kenneth L. Garrett is an independent photographer with a Bachelor of Arts degree in anthropology from the University of Virginia. Specializing in photography of archaeology, paleontology, and ancient cultures worldwide, Garrett has over 50 NGS journal and book projects to his credit. His work has been seen in numerous publications, including *National Geographic* Magazine, *Smithsonian*, *Archaeology*, *Fortune*, *Forbes*, *Time*, *Life*, *Audubon*, *National Wildlife*, and *Natural History*.

After riding donkeys and trekking through Jordan's Faynan copper ore district for three days, Dr. Mohammad Najjar leads the group to the border.

Photograph by Kenneth Garrett, National Geographic.

ON BACK COVER

As the expedition members rode their donkeys through the hyperarid desert of the central Negev, they were reminded of this biblical passage: "They set out from Ezion-geber and encamped in the Wilderness of Zin" (Numbers 33:36). Ezion-geber was identified by American archaeologist Nelson Glueck at the site of Tell el-Kheleifeh near Aqaba in Jordan. The Iron Age fortress there played an important role in the copper metal trade that emanated from Khirbat en-Nahas in the Faynan district.

Photograph by Kenneth Garrett, National Geographic.